SHER SHAH

SHER SHAH

EDITED BY JOHN DOWSON

GYAN

Published by

Gyan Publishing House
5, Ansari Road
Daryaganj, New Delhi-110002
Phone: 011-47034999, 9811692060
E-mail: books@gyanbooks.com

Distribution Network
gyanbooks.com
India, USA, Canada, UK, Australia

ISBN: 978-93-6433-518-8 (HB)
First Published, 1871

2nd Impression 2024

Printed at: Gyan Press, Delhi.

SHER SHAH
EDITOR: JOHN DOWSON

THE HISTORY OF INDIA

THE HISTORY OF INDIA

As Told By Its Own Historians

THE MUHAMMADAN PERIOD

THE POSTHUMOUS PAPERS

OF THE LATE

SIR H. M. ELLIOT

Edited by Prof. John Dowson

PUBLISHERS' NOTE.

This volume is a reprint of the thirty-second article of the fourth volume of the original edition of this work.

The article is entitled *Tarikh-i-Sher Shahi* of Abbas Khan, and was translated into English by E. C. Bayley.

"The *Tarikh-i Sher Shahi,*" says the editor in his Preface, "though written in a spirit of eulogy, does not tend to raise the character of Sher Shah, who has enjoyed a reputation apparently above his merits. That he was an able administrator is no doubt true, but the account which this work gives of his regulations and arrangements does not show them to be of a very enlightened order. He was a cautious rather than an enterprising commander, and was more prone to seek success by crafty and crooked courses, than by the exercise of valour and daring. His soldier-like death in the trenches has cast a ray of martial glory upon his memory; but the treacherous betrayal of Bibi Fath Malika of Bengal and the cold-blooded murder of the prisoners of Raisin would bedim a much brighter fame than he achieved."

PRELIMINARY NOTE

These are not the days when the public care to listen to the minor details of an author's life; but Sir H. M. Elliot's relations and the thinned number of his personal friends—while confidently leaving his posthumous works to speak for themselves—recognise the double duty of placing on record the more prominent events of his career, and of defining under what guarantee his writings are now submitted, so to say, to a new generation of readers. The former will be found in a separate note, but to explain the origin and progressive advance of the present publication, it may be stated that after Sir Henry Elliot's death, at the Cape of Good Hope, his fragmentary papers were brought to this country by his widow. And as the introductory volume of the original work had been issued under the auspices and at the cost of the Government of the North-Western Provinces of India, the MSS.—constituting the materials already prepared for the more comprehensive undertaking in thirteen volumes—were placed at the disposal of those ever liberal promoters of Oriental literature, the Directors of the East India Company, by whom they were submitted to a Committee consisting of the late Prof. H. H. Wilson, Mr. Edward Clive Bayley, of the Bengal Civil Service, and Mr. W. H. Morley, of the Inner Temple, a gentleman who had distinguished himself as an Arabic scholar, and who was reputed to be well versed in other branches of Oriental lore. On the recommendation of this Committee, the Court of Directors readily sanctioned a grant of £500 towards the purposes of the publication, and Mr. Morley was himself entrusted with the editorship. Mr. Morley's circumstances, at this critical time, are understood to have been subject to important changes, so that, although he entered upon his task with full alacrity and zeal, his devotion soon slackened, and when the MSS. were returned four years afterwards, they were found to be in such an imperfectly advanced state as effectually to discourage any hasty selection of a new editor. For which reserve, indeed, there were other and more obvious reasons in the paucity of scholars available in this country, who could alike appreciate the versatile knowledge of the author, and do justice to the critical examination of his leading Oriental authorities, or other abstruse texts, where references still remained imperfect.

As Lady Elliot's adviser in this matter, a once official colleague of her husband's, and alike a free participator in his literary tastes, I trust that I have secured the best interests of the projected undertaking in the nomination of Professor J. Dowson, of the Staff College of Sandhurst, who has so satisfactorily completed the first volume, under the revised distribution of the work, now submitted to the public.—EDWARD THOMAS.

CONTENTS.

PREFACE

THIS work was written by order of the Emperor Akbar, and its author bestowed upon it the title 'Tuhfat-i Akbar Shahni;' but Ahmad Yadgar, who wrote the 'Tarikh-i Salatin-i Afghana' a few years afterwards, calls it the 'Tarikh-i Sher Shahi,' and so it continues to be known. The author of the work was 'Abbas Khan, son of Shaikh 'Ali Sarwani. Nothing is known of the author beyond the little which he incidentally mentions in the course of the work, that he was connected by marriage with the family of Sher Shah, and so had peculiar sources of information as to the life and character of that adventurous and successful chief, whose craft and valour won a crown. 'Abbas Khan certainly had high connexions, but he attained no great distinction in his own person. He received the command of 500 horse from the Emperor Akbar, of which, by the intrigues of his enemies, he was soon deprived. This so wounded his feelings that he resolved to "return to the country of his fathers." But the Khan Khanan took compassion on him, and being informed of his own history and that of his ancestors, procured for him "a clear 200 rupees a month", which he appears to have lost soon afterwards.

The work is valuable as the production of a contemporary writer who had excellent means of obtaining information, although its literary merit is but slender. It is a biography, not a history, and its method is one that requires a vigorous and versatile writer. The various actors are made to describe the scenes which occurred

[1] The exact date of its composition is not given, but it was probably soon after 987H (1579 A.D.), a date which is mentioned by the writer in the course of the work when referring to his personal affairs.

under their observation, and to set forth their own views and opinions. This is all done in a very prolix and tedious style without the slightest diversity of character or expression. All the persons concerned talk in the same strain; and their ostensible speeches, and the ordinary narrative of the author, are alike verbose and wearisome. In the following Extracts the expressions of opinion and sentiment have been greatly curtailed, but the narrative and records of events have been left intact. The dates given are few and far between, but there is nothing peculiar in this, as all other works of the period are similarly deficient.

Sher Shah has obtained a great reputation for his administrative ability, and this work has fortunately preserved the means of forming a judgment of his character and talents. Upon this part of the work Sir H. Elliot says: "The conclusion of the work containing the regulations is very valuable, though overlaudatory. The account which he gives of what the governors did and did not, shows a fearful state of existing anarchy. Much of this matter is also given in the 'Waki'at-i Mushtaki' ".

Copies of the work vary very much, and, in some, long passages are omitted. Sir H. Elliot's own copy has been considerably abbreviated, but judgment has not always been shown in the work of excision. Sir H. Elliot is, no doubt, right in remarking "that the most long-winded probably best represent the original." The whole of the translation which follows is the work of E. C. Bayley, B.C.S., who had three manuscripts to work upon, but he appears to have afterwards received and used a fourth copy, "fuller and better, which probably belonged to the Nawab of Tonk." The Editor has had at his command Sir H. Elliot's MS., and a better copy procured by General Cunningham.

Subsequent writers upon this period of history made great use of this work. Ahmad Yadagar and Ni'amatu-llah acknowledged their obligations in the 'Tarikh-i

Salatin-i Afghana', and in the 'Makhzan-i Afghani' translated by Dorn. It has come down to us in an incomplete state, for the second chapter, containing the history of Islam Khan, and the third, containing the history of the princess descended from Sher Shah, are not contained in the known manuscripts; but it seems tolerably certain that they were really written. Ni'amatu-llah (Dorn 151) quotes our author for an anecdote of Islam Khan which is not contained in the first chapter of the work; and Sir H. Elliot thinks that "the prosiness of the Speeches in Dorn seems to render it highly probable that 'Abbas Sarwani is the author of them."

This "first chapter was translated into Urdu by one Mazhar 'Ali Khan, at the request of Captain James Mowatt or Mouat, and in the preface the Marquis of Wellesley and Lord Cornwallis are praised. The translation, which has the title of 'Tarikh-i Sher Shahi,' is easy and flowing."[2] Garcin de Tassy[3] says that a translation into Urdu was made by Mirza Lutf Ali, of Dehli, in 1805, and he adds, "Il semble, d'apres une note de M. Shakespear que cet ouvrage a ete traduit en Anglais," but of this English translation nothing more is known. There is probably some mistake about the name of the Urdu translator, for it is not likely there are two translations. The date 1805 is just the time when the Marquis of Wellesley and Lord Cornwallis would receive a writer's laudation.

The following chronological table was drawn up by Sir H. Elliot, and has not been altered in any way. It differs in some respects from the Table given by Mr. Thomas in his "Chronicles of the Pathan Kings," page 393.

The chronology of this period is very difficult and various. I will put down the dates—the most trustworthy

[2] *Journ. As. Soc., Bengal, 1871, p. 118.*

[3] *Biog. Bibl. Hind, tome i., p. 536.*

are those of Abu-l Fazl. The others each give only a few.

A.H.

932. *Death of Ibrahim.—Price Humayun goes to Jajmau and Jaunpur.*

933. *Recalled.—Takes Kalpi.—Sanka.—Kol.—Mewat.*

934. *Sambal.—Kanauj.—Muhammad 'Ali Jang-Jang against Bayazid. Babar to Chanderi.—Ganges.—Gogra.*

935. *Babar to Gwalior.—After return to Agra.—Again Agra.—Boats on Jumna.—Etawa.—Kora.—Karra.—Chunar.—Benares.—Chaunsa.—Gogra. — Arrives at Agra.*

936. *Humayun returns to Agra.*

937. *Babar dies Jumada 1st.*

938. *Humayun to Kalinjar.*

939. *Humayun to eastward against Ben and Bayazid, Jaunpur and Chunar.*

940. *Humayun builds Dinpanah.—To Bhojpur, where Muhammad Zaman was captured.*

941. *Humayun to Kalpi and Gujarat via Raisin and Sarangpur.*

942. *Gujarat.—Returns to Agra.*

943. *Again to Jaunpur, and then Chunar (Firishta): Delhi, according to Elphinstone, meaning perhaps Agra.*

944. *Jaunpur, Chunar (Elphinstone).*

945. *Humayun takes Gaur, and remains there.*

946. *Chaunsa.—Action on the Ganges, in Safar.—Sher Shah again acquires Bengal and Jaunpur.—Kutb Khan goes to Kalpi, where he is killed. Humayun at Agra.*

947. *Action at Kanauj, in Muharram. Immediate flight from Agra via Dehli and Rohtak to Lahore, where all brothers assemble Rajab 1st, and leave Jumada 2nd.*

948. ——————

949. *Sher Shah to Bengal? Gwalior, Malwa.*

950. *Raisin, Ajmir, Nagor, Maldeo.—As Muharram, 950, began in April, 1543, he may have gone down to Raisin in the hot weather, then returned to Agra and had all next cold season for Rajputana.*

951. *Elphinstone says Marwar in this year. I have disproved him in a note. Chitor and Kalinjar.*

952. *Sher Shah dies, Rajab 1st, at Kalinjar. Much may perhaps be settled by the 'Tabakat-i Akbari,' 'Badauni,' and the 'Tarikh-i Alfi.'*

EXTRACTS

[PRAISE OF GOD AND THE PROPHET]

[4]THE First Chapter contains the history of the reign of Sher Shah Sur. The Second relates the history of the reign of Islam Shah, son of Sher Shah Sur. The Third Chapter concerns the history of the princes who were descended from Sher Shah, and who, subsequent to Islam Khan, laid claim to the sovereignty, and struck coin and read the *khutba* in their own names; and who dethroned the son of Islam Shah.

I, the humble sweeper of the threshold of the dweller in the palace the Second Alexander, the author of the history of the reigns of the Afghans—'Abbas, son of Shaikh 'Ali Sarwani—write by order of the Emperor Akbar.

CHAPTER I

Account of the reign of Sher Shah Sur

I derive my information from trustworthy Afghans, skilled in the science of history and in rhetoric, who accompanied the king from the beginning of his fortunes to the end of his reign, and were employed in his confidential service. I have written also what I have well ascertained from others. Whatever was opposed to the information thus acquired, and could not stand the touchstone of truth, I have rejected.

[4] [This passage is not in Sir H. Elliot's manuscript, in which the mention of Chapter III comes immediately after the doxology.]

When Sultan Bahlol, of the family of Sahu-khail, of the tribe of Lodi Afghan, possessed the throne of Delhi, there were many persons in the various kingdoms of Hind who struck coin, and had the *khutba* read in their own names, and who were hostile to him.

Sultan Mahmud bin Sultan Ibrahim Sharki possessed the throne of Jaunpur, Sultan Mahmud Khilji reigned in Malwa, Sultan Kutbu-d din in Gujarat, Sultan 'Alau-ddin Ahmad Shah in the Dekhin, and Sultan Zainu-l 'abidin in Kashmir; but the names of the rulers of Bengal[5] and Tatta are not known to me. The ruler of Multan was Shaikh Yusuf, the spiritual successor of Shaikh Makhdum Bahau-d din Zakariya Kuraishi. As long as Sultan Bahlol remained within the great city of Dehli, the capital, no one of these Sultans placed the foot of presumption in the plain of opposition.

Rai Sihar Langah, Zamindar of Zabiri,[6] having expelled Shaikh Yusuf from the city of Multan, himself assumed the kingdom, with the title of Sultan Kutbu-d din. Shaikh Yusuf came to Delhi and entreated the Sultan's aid. Sultan Bahlol and his veteran army having accordingly set out for Multan, in company with Shaikh Yusuf, Sultan Mahmud of Jaunpur came to Dehli and besieged it.

Sultan Bahlol was at Dipalpur when he heard the distressing intelligence of the siege of Dehli, and he said to his nobles and ministers: "The countries of Hind are broad and rich, and their kings are of Indian extraction. In my own land I have many kinsmen renowned for their valour and strength, who are pressed for a live-

[5] The writer of Gen. Cunningham's manuscript remarks that this is an extraordinary statement, considering that the author, in the course of his work, gives the history of the wars of Sher-Shah and his sons with the kings of Bengal.

[6] "Bari," Gen. Cunningham's manuscript.

lihood. Were they here they would be relieved from the contempt of poverty, and I could grasp Hind and destroy my enemies."

His chiefs replied: ".... It is expedient under present circumstances that His Majesty the Sultan should send letters to the chiefs of the tribes in the Roh country to this effect: 'God in his goodness has granted the kingdom of Dehli to the Afghans, but the other kings of Hind wish to expel them from the country. The honour of our women is concerned; the lands of Hind are broad and rich, and can afford maintenance to many. Come, then, to this country; the name indeed of sovereignty shall remain with me, but whatever countries we may conquer shall be shared between us as brothers. Sultan Mahmud of Jaunpur is now besieging Dehli, where the families of the Afghans are. If you feel disposed to assist me, you must do so now, and with a large force.' " .... The king, approving of this advice, issued *farmans* to the chiefs of the various Afghan tribes. On receipt of the *farmans,* the Afghans of Roh came, as is their wont, like ants and locusts, to enter the king's service.

When they drew near to Dehli, a force was sent by Sultan Mahmud Sharki to give them battle. Fath Khan Hirawi, Sipah-salar of Sultan Mahmud, had with him a large force, and elephants like mountains; but the Afghans, in a moment, overthrew his army and levelled it with the dust. When Sultan Mahmud heard of the death of Fath Khan, he fled without fighting, and of the countries of Hind a considerable portion fell on this occasion into the possession of Sultan Bahlol.

Kalu Khan, chief of the Mahmud-khail, of the family of Sahu-khail Bahloli, was wounded in the engagement above mentioned, and Sultan Bahlol sent him a present of money by way of recompense; but he refused it, saying, "I did not come here to sell my wounds." At the same time, many of the chiefs of name besought the king for leave to depart. The king entreated them to remain, but they said: "We came on this occasion to succour and assist you, to save the reputation and honour of your women. Dismiss us now we entreat of you, hereafter we will again return to your service." The king loaded them with presents of money and goods of all kinds, beyond their utmost expectations, and provided them with everything they could possibly want. Such Afghans as chose to remain in his service he ennobled, and gave them *jagirs* to their full content. Kalu Khan, however, said: "Your Majesty must excuse my declining to accept anything, as I did not come to this country from any worldly motives."

When the chiefs of the tribes of Roh had gone, the king commanded his nobles, saying: "Every Afghan who comes to Hind from the country of Roh to enter my service, bring him to me. I will give him a *jagir* more than proportioned to his deserts, and such as shall content him; but if he for reasons of kindred or friendship prefers remaining in the service of any one of you, do you provide for him to his satisfaction; for if I hear of one Afghan from Roh returning thither again for want of a livelihood or employment, I will resume the *jagirs* of that noble who may have refused to entertain him." When the Afghans of Roh heard of this, and saw the favour and affection of the king towards them, they began every day, every month, and every year, to arrive in Hind, and received *jagirs* to their heart's content.

It was at the time of this bounty of Sultan Bahlol, that the grandfather of Sher Shah, by name Ibrahim Khan Sur[7] with his son Hasan Khan, the father of Sher Shah, came to Hindustan from Afghanistan, from a place

[7] The Sur represent themselves as descendants of Muhammad Sur, one of the princess of the house of the Ghorians, who left his native country, and married a daughter of one of the Afghan chiefs of Roh.

which is called in the Afghan tongue "Shargari,"[8] but in the Multan tongue "Rohri." It is a ridge, a spur of the Sulaiman Mountains, about six or seven kos in length, situated on the banks of the Gumal. They entered into the service of Muhabbat Khan Sur, Daud Sahu-khail, to whom Sultan Bahlol had given in *jagir* the *parganas* of Hariana and Bahkala, etc. in the Panjab, and they settled in the *pargana* of Bajwara.

Sher Shah was born in the reign of Sultan Bahlol, and they named him Farid Khan.[9]

After some time had elapsed, Ibrahim Khan left Muhabat Khan and entered the service of Jamal Khan Sarang-khani, of Hisar-Firozah, who bestowed on him several villages in *pargana* Narnaul for the maintenance of forty horsemen. And Mian Hasan Khan, the father of Farid Khan, entered the service of Masnad-i-'ali 'Umar Khan Sarwani Kalkapur, who bore the title of Khan-i 'azam, and was a counsellor and courtier of Sultan Bahlol. After the death of Masnad-i 'ali Tatar Khan, Bahlol gave (the government of) Lahore to this 'Umar Khan, who held as *jagirs* in the *sirkar* of Sirhind, Bhatnur, Shahabad, and Paelpur; and 'Umar Khan gave several villages in the *pargana* of Shahabad as a *jagir* to Hasan Khan.

After some time, Farid Khan said to his father Hasan Khan, "Take me before Masnad-i 'ali 'Umar Khan, and say for me: 'Farid Khan wishes to serve you—order him on any duty of which he is capable.' " Hasan Khan declined compliance on account of his tender age, recommending him to wait some time longer. Farid Khan then spoke to his mother, and his mother said to Hasan Khan—"Since he desires to see the Masnad-i 'ali, take him with you—perhaps he may be pleased at the request of so young a boy, and give him something." Hasan

[8] Var. "Zaghari," "Zhaghari,"

[9] The *Tarikh-i Khan Jahan Lodi* (MS. p. 151) says he was born in Hisar Firozah.

Khan, to please Farid and his mother took him with him before Masnad-i 'ali Umar Khan and said: "Farid wishes to serve you." 'Umar Khan replied—"Farid is now a little boy; when he is fit for my service I will employ him. For the present I give him Balhu, a hamlet of the village of Mahawali."[10] Hasan Khan and Farid Khan were exceedingly delighted and when Farid got home he said to his mother—"My father would not take me but at your request, and Masnad-i-'ali has given me a village in *pargana* Shahabad."

Several years after this, Ibrahim Khan, the father of Hasan Khan, died at Narnaul. Hasan Khan, when he heard of his father's death, left Shahabad, and coming before 'Umar Khan, who was with Sultan Bahlol's army, requested leave of absence to condole with the members of his father's family and retainers, saying he would return with them, for that he would not quit 'Umar Khan's service for any worldly advancement. 'Umar Khan replied: "You are aware that I have already given you your share of the *jagirs* which I possess, nor can I entertain more men. Your father's retainers now all look to you. You will be able to obtain your father's *jagir*, or even a larger one than your father's was. I am not so unjust to my own tribe as to keep you on a small *jagir*." Such were the Afghan nobles, and such their favour towards their own race and kindred, that if they saw their Afghans could elsewhere obtain more than they themselves were able to give, they at once sent them with recommendations in search of better employment.

Hasan Khan was well pleased, and the next day Masnad-i 'ali sent for Jamal Khan and strongly recommending Hasan Khan to him persuaded him to bestow on him his father's *jagir*, with several villages in addition to it, and said, "Whatever kindness you show to Hasan Khan, you will be doing a favour to me." Then giving

[10] Var. "Hani."

Hasan Khan a horse and a dress of honour, he dismissed him. After this, Hasan Khan did such service for Jamal Khan as satisfied and pleased him.

After Sultan Bahlol's death, Sikandar his son succeeded, and conquered Jaunpur from his brother Baibak, and conferred the *subah* on Jamal Khan, and ordered him to keep up 12,000 horse, and to assign them *jagirs.* Jamal Khan, who was much pleased with Hasan Khan's good service, took him with him, and gave him in *jagir* the *parganas* of Sahsaram, Hajipur and Tanda,[11] near Benares, to maintain 500 horsemen.

Hasan Khan had eight sons. Farid Khan and Nizam Khan were born of one Afghan mother; 'Ali and Yusuf of another mother; Khurram[12] and Shadi Khan of a third; Sulaiman and Ahmad of a fourth.

Hasan Khan did not care for or love the mother of Farid and Nizam, but was very fond of his slave-girls, and was especially attached to the mother of Sulaiman and Ahmad; and she gained such influence over Hasan Khan, that she entirely ruled him. Angry words often passed between Hasan and Farid. When he was assigned *jagirs,* Mian Hasan showed little partiality to Farid, and did not give him a jagir which contented him. Farid Khan, annoyed with his father, went to Jamal Khan at Jaunpur. When Mian Hasan discovered that Farid had gone there, he wrote to Jamal Khan thus: "Farid Khan, being annoyed with me, has gone to you without sufficient cause. I trust in your kindness to appease him, and send him back; but if refusing to listen to you, he will not return I trust you will keep him with you, for I wish him to be instructed in religious and polite learning."

[11] The other historians, as Nia'matu-lla, are more specific and call it Khaspur Tanda, which is one of the *parganas* attached to the *sirkdar* of Jaunpur.

[12] Some copies, as well as the *Makhzan-i Afghani,* read Mudahir instead of Khurram, and make him own brother to Sulaiman and Ahmad.

Jamal Khan sent for Farid, and advised him in every possible way to return to his father; but he refused, and said, "If my father wants me back to instruct me in learning, there are in this city many learned men: I will study here." Jamal Khan made no further objection. Farid employed himself in studying Arabic at Jaunpur. He also studied thoroughly the *Kafia,*[13] with the commentaries of Kazi Shahabu-d din, and the biographies of most of the kings of ancient times. He had got by heart the *Sikandar-nama,* the *Gulistan,* and *Bostan.* etc., and was also reading the works of the philosophers. Subsequently, whenever, during his reign, learned men came to ask him for maintenance (*madad-ma'ash*), he used to ask them about the *Hashia-i Hindia,* and he still retained his liking for books of history and the lives of ancient kings.

It happened after some years, that Hasan Khan came to Jamal Khan, when all his kinsmen who were in Jaunpur reproached him for having sent Farid away from his presence for the sake of a slave-girl; and they remarked that Farid Khan, young as he was, gave promise of a future greatness; that he bore the marks of excellence on his forehead, and that in all the tribe of Sur there was none who possessed learning, talent, wisdom, and prudence like him; and he had qualified himself so well, that if Hasan Khan would entrust him with the charge of a *pargana,* he would discharge it excellently well, and perfectly perform all his duties. Hasan Khan assented to what his kindred said, and replied, "Pacify him and bring him to me; I will agree to whatever you say." His friends replied, "As you are generally in Jaunpur in attendance on Jamal Khan, it is advisable you should entrust the administration of your two *parganas* to Farid." Hasan Khan agreed to his kinsmen's request. In great glee they came to Farid, and said, "Mian Hasan

[13] A work on grammar.

has agreed to everything we have said in your behalf, and has dissented from nothing. It behoves you also to assent to what we say to you." Farid Khan replied, "I will agree to anything you may say, nor will I ever draw back from it; but as soon as Hasan Khan sees the face of the slave-girl, he will do whatever she tells him." His kinsmen rejoined: "Do you nevertheless agree; if he departs from his agreement with us, we will remonstrate with him."

When Farid heard these words of his kinsmen, he said, "To please you I accept the management of the two districts. I will not fail to do my duty to the best of my power." Farid Khan, much pleased, accompanied his relatives to his father's presence. His father also was much gratified, and kept him for some months with him. Afterwards, Hasan Khan wished to send Farid to the *parganas;* but Farid representing to Hasan Khan that he wished first to speak with him, he obtained leave to do so, and thus began: "Many soldiers and subordinates, our kinsmen, have *jagirs* in these *parganas.* I shall devote myself to increase the prosperity of the district, and that depends on a just administration; for it has been said by the learned:" . . . . When Hasan Khan heard his son's speech he was much gratified, and said: "I will give you the power both to grant and to resume the soldier's *jagirs,* and I will not reverse anything you may do." He accordingly sent Farid Khan to his two *parganas* with every mark of favour.

When he got to his *jagirs,* he said: "Let all the head men, (*mukaddaman*) and the cultivators (*muzari'an*) on whose labour the prosperity of the district depends, and all the village accountants (*patwaris*), attend my presence. When they came, he summoned also the soldiery, and thus addressed them: "My father (*abu*) has committed to me the power of appointing and dismissing you. I have set my heart on improving the prosperity of the district, in which object also your own interests are concerned; and by this means I hope to establish my reputation." . . . . When he had finished exhorting the soldiery, he turned to the peasantry, and said: "This day I give you your choice as to your mode of payment. Do whatever is most advantageous to your own interests in every possible way."

Some of the head-men asked for written agreements for a fixed money rent;[14] others preferred payment in kind (*kismat-i ghalla*). Accordingly he gave leases and took agreements, and fixed the payments for measuring the fields (*jaribana*), and the fees for the tax-collectors and measurers (*muhassilana*); and he said to the *Chaudharis* and head-men: "I know well that the cultivation depends on the humble peasants, for if they be ill off they will produce nothing, but if prosperous they will produce much. I know the oppressions and exactions of which you have been guilty towards the cultivators; and for this reason I have fixed the payments for measurements, and the tax-gatherers' fees,—that if you exact from the cultivators more on this account than is fixed, it may not be credited to you in making up your accounts. Be it known to you, that I will take the accounts of the fees in my own presence. Whatever dues are rightly taken I will sanction, and compel the cultivators to pay them; and I will also collect the government dues for the autumn harvest in the autumn, and for the spring harvest in the spring; for balances of Government dues are the ruin of a *pargana,* and the cause of quarrels between the cultivators and the Government officers. It is right for a ruler to show leniency to the cultivators at the period of measurement, and to have a regard to the actual produce; but when the time of payment comes he should show no leniency, but collect the revenue with all strictness. If he pperceives the cultivators are evading

[14] In two copies *jarib;* in one, *patta-kabuliyat.*

payment, he should so chastise them as to be an example to others not to act in the same way." He then said to the peasantry: "Whatever matter you have to represent, bring it always yourselves to me. I will suffer no one to oppress you."

Having thus addressed them, he dismissed them with honorary dresses to carry on their cultivation. After dismissing the cultivators, he said to his father's officers: "The cultivators are the source of prosperity. I have encouraged them and sent them away, and shall always watch over their condition, that no man may oppress and injure them; for if a ruler cannot protect humble peasantry from the lawless, it is tyranny to exact revenue from them. There are certain *zamindars* who have been behaving contumaciously in these *parganas*, who have not presented themselves at the Governor's court (*mahkama-i-hakim*), do not pay their full revenue, and harass the villages in their neighbourhood—how shall I overcome and destroy them?" They replied: "Most of the troops are with Mian Hasan; wait a few days and they will return." Farid said, "I cannot have patience while they refuse to come to me, and continue to oppress and injure the people of God; do you consider what I can contrive against these rebels, and how I may chastise them."

He ordered his father's nobles to saddle 200 horses, and to see how many soldiers there were in the *pargana* and he sent for all the Afghans and men of his tribe who were without *jagirs*, and said to them,—"I will give you subsistence and clothing till Mian Hasan returns. Whatever goods or money you may get from the plunder of these rebels is yours, nor will I ever require it of you; and whoever among you may distinguish himself for him I will procure a good jagir from Mian Hasan. I will myself give you horses to ride on." When they heard this they were much pleased, and said they would not fail in doing their duty under his auspices. He put the men who had engaged to serve him in good humour by all sorts of favours, and by gifts of clothes, etc. and presented them also with a little money.

He then sent to the cultivators for horses, saying, "Bring your horses to me as a loan for a few days, as I particularly require them. When I return after finishing this business, I will give you back your horses." They willingly and cheerfully agreed to lend their horses, and from every village they brought one or two horses, and put on the saddles which they had ready in their houses, etc. Farid gave to every one of his soldiers who had not one of his own, a horse to ride, and hastened against the rebels, and plundered their villages, bringing away the women and children, cattle and property. To the soldiery he made over all the property and quadrupeds which came into their possession; but the women and children and the peasantry he kept himself in confinement, and sent to the head-men, saying: "Pay me my rights; if not, I will sell your wives and children, and will not suffer you to settle anywhere again. Wherever you may go, thither will I pursue you; and to whatever village you may go, I will command the head-men to seize and make you over to me, or else I will attack them also." When the head-men heard these words, they sent to say: "Pardon our past offences, and if hereafter we do anything you do not approve, punish us in any way you choose." Farid Khan sent to say in reply, "Give security, in order that if you offend and abscond, your security may be held responsible for your appearance." So the head-men, whose wives and families he had in confinement, paid what was due from them to Government and gave security for their appearance, and so released their wives and families.

There were some *zamindars* who had committed all sorts of offences, such as theft and highway robbery, and refusing to pay revenue, never came to the Governor's presence, but were insolent from confidence in their numbers. Although these were often warned, they took no heed. Farid Khan collected his forces, and commanded that every one of his villagers who had a horse should come riding upon it, and that he who had not a horse should come on foot. And he took with him half his own soldiers, and the other half he employed in collecting revenue and other local duties.

When the soldiers and peasantry were asssembled, he marched towards the villages of the recusants, and at a distance of a kos threw up an earthen entrenchment; and ordered them to cut down the neighbouring jungle. His horsemen he directed to patrol round the villages; to kill all the men they met, and to make prisoners of the women and children, to drive in the cattle, to permit no one to cultivate the fields, to destroy the crops already sown, and not to permit any one to bring anything in from the neighbouring parts, nor to allow any one of them to carry anything out of the village, and to watch them day and night; and he every day repeated the order to his force to invest the village, and not to permit a soul to go out. His footmen he also ordered to cut down the jungle. When the jungle was all cut down, he marched from his former position, and made another entrenchment nearer the village, and occupied it. The rebels were humbled, and sent a representative saying, that if Farid Khan would pardon their fault, they would submit. Farid Khan replied that he would not accept their submission, and that there could be nothing but hostility between him and them; to whichever God might please, he would give the victory.

Although the rebels humbled themselves in every way, and offered to pay a large sum of money, yet Farid Khan would not accept the money, but said to his men: "This is the way of these rebels; first they fight and oppose their rulers: if they find him weak, they persist in their rebelliousness; but if they see that he is strong, they come to him deceitfully and humble themselves, and agree to pay a sum of money, and so they persuade their ruler to leave them alone; but as soon as they find an opportunity, they return to their evil ways....

Early in the morning, Farid Khan mounted and attacked the criminal *zamindars,* and put all the rebels to death, and making all their women and children prisoners, ordered his men to sell them or keep them as slaves; and brought other people to the village and settled them there. When the other rebels heard of the death, imprisonment, and ruin of these, they listened to wisdom, repented of their contumacy, and abstained from theft and robbery.

If any soldier or peasant had a complaint, Farid would examine it in person, and carefully investigate the cause, nor did he ever give way to carelessness or sloth.

In a very short time, both *parganas* became prosperous and the soldiery and peasantry were alike contented. When Mian Hasan heard of this, he was much pleased; and in all companies used to make mention of the prosperity of his *parganas,* the gallantry of his son, and the subjection of the *zamindars.*

The fame of Farid's wisdom was noised abroad over the kingdom of Bihar, and all the nobles of that country who heard of it praised it. He gained a reputation among men, and satisfied and pleased all his friends and others, except a few enemies, such as the mother of Sulaiman.

When after some time, Mian Hasan came to his home from attendance on Masnad-i 'ali Mian Jamal Khan, all the vassals and soldiery with one voice unanimously proclaimed their well-being, and he witnessed himself the prosperity of the country and replenishment of the treasury, and was extremely delighted with Farid. The dislike which he formerly entertained was dispelled, and he distinguished both brothers with all kinds of favours. "I am now old," he said, "nor can I bear the labour and trouble and thought of governing the *par-*

ganas and the soldiery while I live; do you manage them."

This speech displeased Sulaiman and his mother, and they made all kinds of lying and false complaints to Mian Hasan, and the money which Farid had, for his sister's wedding, given to Sulaiman, they changed, and showed to Mian Hasan, declaring it was bad. Every day they complained and railed against Farid Khan, but but Mian Hasan gave ear to none of them. Sulaiman and his mother perceived that Mian Hasan was not incensed against Farid by their lying complaints, but said to them, "It is not right that you should always rail at Farid. Except you two, there is not a person among my friends, soldiers, or vassals, who complains of him; and I also am satisfied and grateful for his conduct and excellent behaviour, for both my *parganas* are prosperous."

When the mother of Sulaiman heard Mian Hasan thus speak, she was overcome with grief, and discontinued complaining to Mian Hasan, but from that day seldom held any intercourse with Mian Hahan. She publicly displayed her grief, and the love and the intimacy which Mian Hasan had previously enjoyed with her were interrupted. Mian Hasan perceived her great affliction, and one day said to her, "What is the cause of your grief? and what is the reason of your shunning me?" She replied, "I was once your humble slave, you distiguished me by your love and affection, and the rest of your family, from envy, are little affectionate towards me; nor yet, to the best of my ability, have I failed in my duty to them. He (Farid) is your eldest son, and looks to succeed to your position, and if, during your life, you do not distinguish my sons as well as Farid, nor give them the management of a *pargana,* I will in your presence kill myself and my sons; for in your lifetime they should acquire property. Farid and your kindred, who are my enemies, after your death will insult and turn us out of the *parganas.* Therefore, it is better for us to die in your presence, than to survive dishonoured among our enemies."

Mian Hasan, bound in the chain of her love, and helpless from the force of his affection (from which to the lover there is no escape), was persuaded by her, and withdrew his fickle affections from his eldest sons, and sought to remove him from the country, and to place his other sons in his room. The mother of Sulaiman said, "I hope much from your love, but your relatives will not permit you to take away the management of the *parganas* from Farid." Mian Hasan, who was entangled in the noose of her love, swore a solemn oath to her and appeased her.

After this Mian Hasan sought to discover some fault in Farid, and to remove him, and employed himself in examining his actions. Excessive aversion was kindled and angry words passed between Mian Hasan and Farid. When Farid discovered that Mian Hasan had promised the mother of Sulaiman that he would give the management of both parganas to her sons, and had violated the promise which he had given to his kinsmen, Farid threw up the management of them, and sent to Mian Hasan, saying, "So long as I saw my father's affections and kindness turned towards me, I carried on the business of the *parganas*—now make anybody manager you like. Certain persons from envy and enmity have conveyed to your hearing reports which have grieved you. My father, inquire into them, as I shall show you how." . . .

Mian Hasan sent to Farid in reply, saying, "There is no reason that I should make inquiries; for while I was even absent with the army, I understood the real state of the *parganas*, and that you doubled the prosperity of the country. And if you have appropriated anything well and good. It is your own property, and it is no reproach. . . . . Your degenerate brothers, Sulaiman and the rest, give me daily annoyance. I do not think they are able to manage the country. However much I advise, it makes no impression on them; they have taken away my rest and peace, and their mother is interfering perpetually in my affairs on behalf of her sons. I am obliged to permit Sulaiman and Ahmad to act for a short time as *shikkdars* of the *parganas,* that I may be freed from this daily and nightly vexation." When Farid heard these words from his father, he said, "The two parganas are my father's, let him give their management to whomsoever he will."

When Mian Hasan's relations heard that he had taken away the management of the two *parganas* from Farid, and was intending to confer it on Sulaiman and Ahmad, and that Farid was preparing to go to Agra to gain his livelihood (for in those days Agra was the capital city), they came to Mian Hasan, and said: "It is not right for you to take away the management of the *parganas* from his son, and give it to Sulaiman and Ahmad; for Farid, by his care has doubled their prosperity, and has so established his authority in them, as no one ever before did, nor has he committed any fault for which he ought to be removed. It is not right to quarrel with such an able son in your old age; especially in these times, when the authority of Sultan Ibrahim is shaken, and every Afghan of influence is aiming at power and independence."

Mian Hasan replied to his relatives, "I know it is not right to grieve Farid; but what can I do? for Sulaiman and his mother have driven me into a strait, nor do they give me a moment's rest. . . . I am an old man, the time of my death is near at hand. I cannot break my promise. I give the management of the *parganas* to Sulaiman and Ahmad during my life. If they govern well, so that the *parganas* prosper, the people are happy, and the soldiery content, well and good; for then during my lifetime they will acquire a good name; for thus Farid has gained a name among men, and has gladdened my heart. Wheresoever he may go, he will be able to gain his own livelihood. But if they prove unfit, they will (at any rate) be for some time during my life laying up worldly goods. Of this I am certain, that after my death the government of the *parganas* will be conferred on Farid, who is deserving of it." . . . . .

When his kinsmen heard this reply of Mian Hasan, they said, "You send Farid away from you to please a slave-girl! It is wrong in these times to stir up strife for a slave-girl's sake. For from the proceedings of the Lohanis in Bihar, it appears that they will shortly throw off the king's yoke and declare their independence. It has been said, 'it is wrong to place confidence in women,'" etc. . . . . But in spite of what his relatives said, Mian Hasan, who was a captive in the bonds of his love for the slave-girl, did not assent to their representation.

When Farid entertained no longer any hope from Mian Hasan, he took leave of his friends, and set off for Agra, by way of Kahnpur (Cawnpore), which *pargana* then belonged to the *jagir* of 'Azim Humayun Sarwani, who there maintained a large number of followers. Most of the Sarwanis were settled in that neighbourhood. When Farid reached Kahnpur, the Sarwanis who were connected by marriage with Mian Hasan entertained Farid. Among them, one Shaikh Ismail was present. Farid asked who he was. The Sarwanis at first said that he was a Sarwani; but afterwards that he was a Sur of Farid's own tribe, but that his mother was a Sarwani. Farid said to him, "Why did you not tell me you were a Sur?" Shaikh Ismail said, "I did not tell you that I was a Sarwani, but if they said so, what fault is it of mine?" Farid said to Shaik Ismail, "Come with me." Shaikh Ismail and Ibrahim both accompanied Farid, and in the battle in which Farid defeated Kutb Shah, King of Bengal, Ismail greatly distinguished himself. Habib Khan Kakar, who was his sister's son and lived in his house, slew Kutb Shah with an arrow, and as Habib Khan was a follower of Shaikh Ismail, the latter got the credit of having killed Kutb Shah. On that occasion, Farid gained the surname of Sher Shah, and he bestowed that of Shuja'at Khan on Shaikh Ismail. When Sher Shah Sur gained the kingdom of Hindustan, he bestowed the government of Mandu on him, and gave to Ibrahim Khan, who also attained to great consideration, the title of Sarmast Khan.

It so happened that when Farid arrived at Agra, Daulat Khan, the son of Budhu (who had been brought up in Azim Humayun Sarwani's house), held the command of 12,000 horse, and was in great favour with Sultan Ibrahim. Farid Khan chose Daulat Khan for his patron, and did him such good service that Daulat Khan often said: "I am ashamed to look Farid Khan in the face; if he will only say what I can do for him, I will not fail to use my utmost endeavours to accomplish his desire, only let him say what he wants."

When Farid understood that Daulat Khan took an interest in his affairs, he wrote saying, "Mian Khan is old, and his senses are failing him, and he is spell-bound and infatuated with a Hindu slave-girl. Whatever she tells him he does, and has permitted her to manage his districts, and she has trampled on all his relatives and disgusted his soldiery and the people he rules. Both *parganas* are falling to ruin from the folly of this slave-woman. If the king will confer on me the two *parganas*. I and my brother will, with 500 horse, serve him in any place or way he orders, in addition to the service Mian Hasan now renders. When Daulat Khan heard his request, he encouraged him in every possible way, and said, "Be of good heart, for I will tell the king the truth about Mian Hasan, and will get the *parganas* taken from your father and given to you."

Daulat Khan, on representing the state of Mian Hasan's case to the king, said: "Farid is the ablest of his sons, and has long managed the *parganas*. The soldiery and inhabitants are content with him. If the king will bestow on him the management of the two *parganas,* he and his brother will do whatever duty you may command with 500 horse." The king replied, "He is a bad man who complains against and accuses his own father." Daulat Khan informed Farid, and said: "This reply came from the king's own mouth, but do not you be cast down. God willing, I will get for you the management of these two *parganas,* and will, moreover, watch over your interests." When Farid heard the matter, he was grieved, but to please Daulat Khan remained with him. He assisted Farid with money, and indeed gave him such a daily allowance as to enable him to accumulate somewhat.

After some time, Mian Hasan died. On the third day after his death Sulaiman placed Mian Hasan's turban on his own head, and was sitting among his friends when Mian Nizam came, accompanied by his partisans, and took the turban from off Sulaiman's head, saying, "It does not become you, in the absence of your elder brother, who is celebrated for every excellent quality, and is on service with the king, to place the turban of Mian Hasan on your own head. Have a fear of God! Have you no shame before the people of the Lord, that you thus act in contravention of law and custom, and create a cause of contention?

During out father's life you acted ungenerously to Farid through your mother's influence; on my father's account I could say nothing. Had it been otherwise, your strength and courage should have been tried; but now such conduct is no longer right. It behoves you to act to Farid in a very different manner from what you have in times past; and abandon strife, for it is not good to contend with your elder brother. Mian Hasan in his lifetime assigned separate *jagirs* to his sons; be content with this, and resign your superiority; for it is your elder brother's right. If you will not give up fighting, you will become dependent on others; nor will any one speak well of you. Contention will only get you a bad name and ruin the *parganas*." Sulaiman said, "If my brother treats me with any kindness, I cannot choose but serve him."

After this Mian Nizam wrote to Farid, telling him of the death of Mian Hasan, and of the whole affair. When Farid got the news, he performed the usual mourning, and told Daulat Khan the posture of affairs as regarded Sulaiman. Daulat Khan said "Do not be anxious. Please God, the king will give you the government of the two *parganas*. Daulat Khan told the king the news of Mian Hasan's death, and procuring *farmans* for the two *parganas*, gave them to Farid, and procured him also leave to go to his *jagir*, that he might establish his possession and authority over them, and console his family and followers; after which he was again to present himself before the king. When Farid arrived, all his relations and all the soldiery came out to meet him, and yielded obedience to the *farman*. Sulaiman, unable to oppose him, went away to Muhammad Khan Sur Daud-Shah-khail, governor of the *pargana* of Chaundh, etc., who commanded 1,500 horse. As there had been some little ill-feeling between this Muhammad Khan and Hasan Khan, he desired nothing better than that the brothers should quarrel, and both become dependent on him. He said to Sulaiman. "Have practice for a short while, for Farid has got a royal *farman* for the government. But Sultan Ibrahim has maltreated the nobles of Sultan Bahlol and Sultan Sikandar, and they have all retired to their own districts, and remain there. And the Khan-khanan Yusuf-khail, who was governor of the Panjab, etc. has sent his son Dilawar Khan to Kabul, to fetch the Emperor Babar, and he is now coming back with the Mughals. There will be war between the two monarchs. If Sultan Ibrahim prevails, you must go to him, and I will write to him on your behalf and describe Farid as hostile to Mian Hasan, as well as yourself, and that Mian Hasan preferred you. Whatever assistance your fortune gives you, you will get; and if the Mughals conquer, I will by force take the *parganas* from Farid, and and give them to you." Sulaiman replied, "I have taken refuge with you from fear of Farid. Because there is none like you in the tribe of Sur, I place myself in your hands." Shortly after Muhammad Khan sent his *vakil* to Farid with his message: "Listen to my advice, and have respect to my interference. I come to mediate between you; whichever of you declines my mediation will bring shame on his kindred." Farid Khan wrote in reply, "You are, indeed, very great and powerful, and the Daud-Shah-khail is the most exalted among the tribes of Sur; the chieftaincy of the tribe is therefore yours of right. . . The truth is not hid from you, my lord; which is, that in my father's lifetime he was always disputing with me. Even after his death, I offered to give my three brothers a larger *jagir* than had been assigned to them during my father's lifetime, and I said to Sulaiman, 'Let us put aside the ill-feeling that existed between us during our father's life, and let us pass the rest of our lives in amity and affection.' . . . I. send my brother Nizam to bring him to me, and I will give him such a *jagir* as will satisfy him; but let him put aside the desire of sharing as his portion in (the government of) my *pargana;* for while I live he shall never obtain this. " When Muhammad Khan's *vakil* reported what Farid Khan had said and written, Muhammad Khan said to Sulaiman, "Farid Khan will not give you a share quietly. I will make him do so by force. . . .

Sulaiman was much delighted; but the matter was reported to Farid Khan, who consulted with his brother Nizam and his other adherents, and said "I must ally myself with some one who will be able to oppose Muhammad Khan, and there is no one within reach except Bihar Khan, son of Darya Khan Lohani. However, it is best to wait a little. If Sultan Ibrahim prevails, no one will be able to say a word against me; for do I not hold the Sultan's *farman*? And if (which God avert) the Mughals should defeat Sultan Ibrahim, then indeed I must of necessity ally myself to Bihar Khan, and remain in his service." After some time news came that the two monarchs had joined battle on the field of Panipat, and that after a severe contest Sultan Ibrahim had been slain, and that the kingdom of Dehli had fallen into the hands of the Emperor Babar, in the year 932. . . . .

Farid Khan, being thus compelled, went to Bihar Khan, and entered into his service, and employed himself day and night in his business; nor did he rest one moment from it, and from this good service he gained Bihar Khan's favour; so that he had access to him in public and in private, and became one of his most intimate friends. In consequence of his excellent arrangements, he became celebrated throughout the country of Bihar. One day he went out hunting with Bihar Khan, and a tiger (*sher*) having been started, Farid Khan slew it. Bihar Khan, who on the death of Sultan Ibrahim had assumed the title of "Sultan Muhammed," and had caused coin to be struck, and the *khutba* to be read in his own name throughout the country of Bihar, gave to Farid Khan, on account of this gallant encounter, the title of "Sher Khan" and made him the deputy to his son Jalal Khan.

He performed the duties of deputy for a long time, but at length went on leave to visit his own *parganas*, where he delayed for some time. On account of his long absence, Sultan Muhammad used to talk reproachfully of him, and said, "Sher Khan promised to return very shortly, but has remained a long time away." Those were days of confusion, no man put entire confidence in another.

Muhammad Khan Sur same to Sultan Muhammad and spoke detractingly of Sher Khan, saying, "He sees some probability of the advent of Sultan Mahmud, the son of Sultan Sikandar, to whom many of the nobles and Afghans have given in their adhesion. If Your Majesty commands me, I will contrive to bring Farid Khan here without any stir. His brother Sulaiman is an able young man to whom Hasan Khan during his lifetime made over the management of both his *parganas,* when he banished Sher Khan from his districts, who even formerly preferred an accusation against his own father, and of whom the Sultan said, 'This is a bad man who complains even against his own father.' When Hasan Khan died, Farid Khan, through his patron Daulat Khan, obtained a grant of both parganas from Sultan Ibrahim. Sulaiman was also desirous of going to Sultan Ibrahim, to show the recommendatory letter which Mian Hasan when dying had written to the Sultan. But disturbances arose, and he was unable to go, and has now come to you to complain of his brother. If Your Majesty will confer these *parganas* on Sulaiman, Farid Khan will very quickly come unto your presence again. It is now long since that Sulaiman, flying from him, sought refuge with me; and if he attains his rights, he will ever be your obliged servant." Sultan Muhammad replied, "He has done me much good service, how can I give away his *jagirs* to another and that for a trifling fault, and without inquiry? However, to please you they shall both bring their cause before you. Both are similarly related to you—do you favour neither. that the right may be established, and the dust of the enmity which exists between them may be allayed."

Muhammad Khan, when he was dismissed, returned to his own *jagir,* and sent Shadi Khan, his confidential servant to Farid Khan with a message to this effect: "It is not right for you to take possession of both *parganas* and to disinherit your brothers, and lay the foundation of strife among your own kindred. I have sent Shadi Khan to you and I hope you will take heed to what he will say to you. Your brothers have now been a long time with me and the laws and customs of the Afghans are no secret to you."

When Shadi came to Sher Khan, and delivered at full length Muhammad Khan's message, Sher Khan replied: "Do you, Shadi Khan, tell the Khan from me, that this is not the Roh country that I should share equally with my brothers. The country of India is completely at the disposal of the king, nor has any one else any share in it, nor is there any regard to elder or younger, or to kindred. Sikander Lodi thus decided: 'If any noble dies, whatever money or other effects he may leave should be divided among his heirs according to the laws of inheritance but his office and his *jagirs* and his military retinue let him confer on whichever of the sons he thinks most able; and in these no one else has a right to share, nor is any remedy open to them.' Whatever goods and money my father left, Sulaiman with my brothers appropriated before he sought refuge with you. Hitherto, out of regard for my relationship to you, I have said nothing; but whenever he may quit you, I shall reclaim my share of my patrimonial inheritance from him. The *jagir* and office were conferred on me by Sultan Ibrahim; in them no one has any share. But I said to my brothers, 'The *jagirs* which you enjoyed in my father's lifetime I will continue, nay increase to you; but no one can participate in my office.' It does not become you to say, 'Give up Tanda and Malhu to Sulaiman.' I will not willingly yield them. If you take them by force, and give them to him, it is in your power to do so. I have not another word to say."

When Shadi returned from Sher Khan, and reported the whole affair to Muhammad Khan, he was much enraged, and said to Shadi, "Take all my forces with you, seize *parganas* Tanda and Malhu, and make them over to Sulaiman and Ahmad. If he resists you, fight him with all your might; and if you defeat and put him to flight, make over both parganas to Sulaiman, and leaving your army to assist him, return to me, lest when he sees Sulaiman with few followers he will attack him."

When this news reached Sher Khan, he wrote to Sukha, his slave (father of Khawas Khan), the *shikkdar* of Tanda and Malhu, near Benares, and with whom the greater part of Sher Khan's forces were, apprising him that Sulaiman, accompanied by Shadi Khan, was advancing against him, and directing him not to yield up Tanda and Malhu without resistance. When the army of Muhammad Khan approached, Sukha came out of the city to meet it. In the engagement which followed, Sukha was slain, and his army were defeated and fled to Sher Khan, at Sahsaram, nor did they even rally there.

Some persons advised Sher Khan to go to Sultan Muhammad, but he did not agree to this, saying, "These are uncertain times, the Sultan will not quarrel with Muhammad Khan for my sake. He will endeavour to bring about some compromise; but it is not my interest to enter into a compromise." Mian Nizam Khan said, "If it be not your interest to make a compromise, I think it will be best to go to Patna; thence, through the intervention of some proper person, to procure an interview with Sultan Junaid Birlas, at Agra, and to offer to enter his service. Perhaps this might afford an opportunity not only of vengeance on Muhammad Khan, but even of driving him out of Chaundh." Sher Khan agreed to this. and went to Patna, and sent an agent to Sultan Junaid, at Agra, saying, "If Sultan Junaid will give me his parole, and promise not to molest me, I will come and wait upon him, and serve him loyally with all my heart and soul." Sultan Junaid agreeing to this, Sher Khan came to him, bringing with him a very large present. Sultan Junaid was much pleased, and gave him the aid of a large force to recover his *parganas*. Muhammad Khan and Sulaiman, unable to resist, fled to the hill of Rohtas, and Sher Khan got possession not only of his own *parganas*, but also of Chaundh and of several *parganas* which had formerly appertained to the crown. To many of the Afghans and his kindred who had fled to the mountains, he wrote, promising to double their former *jagirs,* and said, "The honour of our women is one (to us all); I have accomplished my revenge, and have regained my *parganas.*" Consequent on the acquisition of these *parganas,* many Afghans came to him. When he perceived that many of the Afghans were collecting round him, he became at ease; gaining confidence, he dismissed the army which Sultan Junaid had sent to his aid with very handsome presents. Sher Khan then wrote to Muhammad Khan Sur, the former ruler of Chaundh, who had fled to the hills, to this effect: "Do not let any fear find its way to your heart, but make your mind quite easy, and come and take possession of your *pargana.* I have acquired several parganas which formerly paid revenue to Sultan Ibrahim, and do not covet the possessions of my kindred. This is a time of sedition and misfortunes. Every Afghan who has any forces is coveting my government and country, and it therefore behoves those who have the means in such a time to collect for their aid and assistance soldiery of their own tribe, so as to preserve their own dominion, and even gain fresh territory. This, therefore, is the wisest course; let us put away our former envy and hatred, and in place of it let us plant the young tree of love and kindness in our hearts, that it may bring forth the fruit of friendship; and this may be the means of our collecting our friends, and so of attaining high station and dignity." On receiving Sher Khan's letter, Muhammad Khan came down from the hills, and again took possession of his own *parganas* of Chaundh, etc.; and he and Sher Khan forgave each other their previous enmity; and Muhammad Khan thus came under obligations to Sher Khan.

Sher Khan, being relieved from all apprehension as regarded Muhammad Khan, went to Sultan Junaid Birlas, at Agra, and thence accompanied him to the presence of the Emperor Babar; was admitted to his Court, was present during the affair of Chanderi, and remained for some time amongst the Mughals, and acquainted himself with their military arrangements, their modes of governing, and the character of their nobles. He often said among the Afghans, "If luck aided me, and fortune stood my friend, I could easily oust the Mughals from Hindustan." When people heard him speak thus, they ridiculed him, and used to say behind his back, "What vain boasting is this of Sher Khan's; he talks about a thing far beyond his power."

I, Abbas, the writer of the adventures of Sher Khan, have heard from the mouth of Shaikh Muhammad my own uncle, whose age was nearly eighty years, the following story: "I was at the battle of Chanderi, with the force of the victorious Emperor Babar, the second Faridun, and in attendance on the Khan Khanan Yusufkhail, who brought the Emperor Babar from Kabul, and Shaikh Ibrahim Sarwani said to me, "Come to Sher Khan's quarters, and hear his impossible boastings, which all men are laughing at.' And accordingly we rode over to Sher Khan's quarters. In the course of conversation, Shaikh Ibrahim said: 'It is impossible that the empire should again fall into the hands of the Afghans, and the Mughals be expelled from the country.' Sher Khan replied: 'Shaikh Muhammad, be you witness now between Shaikh Ibrahim and myself, that if luck and fortune favour me, I will very shortly expel the Mughals from Hind, for the Mughals are not superior to the Afghans in battle or single combat; but the Afghans have let the empire of Hind slip from their hands, on account of their internal dissensions. Since I have been amongst the Mughals, and know their conduct in action, I see that they have no order or discipline, and that their kings, from pride of birth and station, do not personally superintend the government, but leave all the affairs and business of the State to their nobles and ministers, in whose sayings and doings they put perfect confidence. These grandees act on corrupt motives in every case, whether it be that of a soldier's, or a cultivator's, or a rebellious *zemindar's*. Whoever has money, whether loyal or disloyal, can get his business settled as he likes by paying for it; but if a man has no money, although he may have displayed his loyalty on a hundred occasions, or be a veteran soldier, he will never gain his end. From this lust of gold they make no distinction between friend and foe, and if fortune extends a hand to me, the Shaikh shall soon see and hear how I will bring the Afghans under my control, and never permit them again to become divided.' "

After some time, Sher Khan waited upon the Emperor one day at an entertainment, when it happened that they placed before him a solid dish, which he did not know the customary mode of eating. So he cut it into small pieces with his dagger, and putting them into his spoon easily disposed of them. The Emperor Babar remarked this, and wondered at Sher Khan's ingenuity, and said to Khalifa, his minister, who was at his elbow, "Keep an eye on Sher Khan; he is a clever man, and the marks of royalty are visible on his forehead. I have seen many Afghan nobles, greater men than he, but they never made any impression on me; but as soon as I saw this man, it entered into my mind that he ought to be arrested, for I find in him the qualities of greatness and the marks of mightiness." When Sultan Junaid took his leave, he had recommended Sher Khan strongly to the minister.[15] Sher Khan had also made him a very handsome present. So he replied to the Emperor: "Sher Khan is without blame, and does not command a sufficient force to become a cause of uneasiness to Your Majesty. If you arrest him, the Afghans who are present with you will all become suspicious, nor will any other Afghan trust your faith and

[15] Mir Khalifa was the elder brother of Sultan Junaid.

promises, and hence will arise disunion." The Emperor was silenced; but Sher Khan sagaciously perceived that the Emperor had spoken something concerning him.

When Sher Khan got to his own quarters, he said to his men: "The Emperor to-day looked much at me, and said something to the minister; and cast evil glances towards me. This is not a fit place for me to remain—I shall go away." Mounting at once, he left the army. Shortly afterwards the king missed Sher Khan from among the courtiers, and sent for him. The man who was despatched in search of him came to his quarters, but Sher Khan was gone. The Emperor said to the *wazir*, "If you had not hindered me, I could have arrested him at once; he is about to do something, God only knows what!"

When Sher Khan reached his *jagir* after leaving the army, he sent a handsome present to Sultan Junaid, and wrote to say, "I was necessitated to quit the king without taking leave. If I had asked for leave, he would not have given it to me. I was compelled to come to my *jagir*, for my brother Nizam wrote to say that Muhammad Khan and Sulaiman had represented to Sultan Muhammad that I had allied myself with the Mughals, by whose aid I had seized their *parganas*, and they offered, if ordered, to retake these districts. Sultan Muhammad, however, gave them no answer. When I heard this news, it was impossible for me to remain where I was. I am His Majesty's grateful servant; I will do whatever he desires."

After this, Sher Khan took counsel with his brother Nizam and others, saying, "I have no longer any confidance in the Mughals, or they in me; I must go to Sultan Muhammad Khan." He decided on this plan, and when he came to Sultan Muhammad in Bihar, the latter was much delighted, for he had had experience of his great talent. He entrusted his son Jalal Khan to him and said: "I make you my son's lieutenant. Do you instruct him with all your care, for he is of tender age." Sher Khan was much pleased, and took great pains in the discharge of his office. When Sultan Muhammad died, his son Jalal Khan succeeded him, whose mother's name was Dudu, a concubine; and being himself very young, his mother Dudu ruled the kingdom, and she made Sher Khan her deputy in the Government of Bihar and its dependencies. After the death of Dudu, Sher Khan also discharged the duties of the State as deputy for Jalal Khan.

An intimate friendship sprang up between Sher Khan and Makhdum 'Alam, ruler of Hajipur, a noble in the service of the King of Gaur and Bengal. The King of Bengal became displeased with Makhdum Alam; for he (the king) having conceived a design of conquering Bihar from the Afghans, despatched Kutb Khan with a large force for that purpose. Sher Khan earnestly and repeatedly remonstrated. . . . . Nevertheless, Kutb Khan gave no heed to his remonstrances. Sher Khan therefore said to his Afghans, "With the Mughals on one side and the army of Bengal on the other, we have no resource save in our own bravery." The Afghans replied, "Be of good cheer, for we will fight to the utmost; we will never yield the field until we either conquer or die, nor will we be ungrateful to those we have served so long." Sher Khan having prepared for a sturdy resistance, met the enemy. A severe action ensued, in which the Bengal army was defeated. In that engagement Shaikh Ismail much distinguished himself, and Kutub Khan and Habib Khan Kakar were with him. Kutb Khan, leader of the Bengal army, was struck by an arrow, and falling off his horse, expired. Shaikh Ismail gained the victory, and Sher Khan bestowed on him the title of Shuja'at Khan.[16] Of the treasure, horses, elephants, etc., which fell into his hands,

[16] *The Tarikh-i Khan-Jahan Lodi* says that when he was appointed governor of Malwa, the people called him "Shujawal Khan."

Sher Khan did not give any part to the Lohanis, and so he became a man of wealth.

The Lohanis were much angered at this, and hostile feelings sprang up between them and Sher Khan; but they did not openly manifest them. Now Makhdum Alam had not assisted Kutb Khan, and as this misfortune had befallen the latter, the King of Bengal sent an army against Makhdum Alam. I, who am the author of the *Tuhfa Akbar Shahi,* reckon among my ancestors Abbas Khan. Very many sons of Abbas Khan were in Sher Khan's service; (or these) he gave to Mian Hasnu the title of Darya Khan. Among the Khan's nobles, none were equal to him, and he had married Sher Khan's own sister. This Darya Khan died in the beginning of Sher Shah's reign. My object in this detail is as follows: Since a connexion exists between Sher Shah and myself, I am thus better acquainted with his history, which I have learnt from my ancestors. To be brief, Sher Khan was prevented by the hostility of the Lohanis from assisting in person Makhdum Alam but he sent Mian Hasnu Khan to his assistance. Makhdum Alam made over all his property and worldly possession to Sher Khan saying, "If I am victorious, I will reclaim my property; if not, better you should have it than any other." Makhdum Alam was killed in battle, but Mian Hasnu Khan returned alive, and Makhdum Alam's property fell to Sher Khan.

The enmity between Sher Khan and the Lohanis increased daily, until the latter at last plotted to kill Sher Khan, and they thus took counsel among themselves, saying, "Sher Khan waits every day upon Jalal Khan with a very small retinue; let us pretend that Jalal Khan is ill. Sher Khan will go inside the palace to inquire after him. When he is returning, and has passed through one gate, and before he reaches the other, let us kill him, while thus inclosed between the two gates of Jalal Khan's palace."

Some of the Lohanis, who were friends and connexions of Sher Khan, having heard of these machinations, told Sher Khan, who, before receiving the news, had, by his own penetration, discovered from the actions and motions of the Lohanis that they meditated some injury to himself. As he was a wise man he said nothing of the matter, but privately took precaution for his own safety; and all the land and property he had recently acquired he expended in enlisting fresh retainers, to whom he gave *jagirs* and maintenance to their heart's content: but to the Lohanis he gave nothing. When he perceived that he had got so large a number of new soldiers collected together that the Lohanis could not injure him or prevail against him in battle, he proclaimed the enmity of Lohanis and said to Jalal Khan, "You well know that the King of Bengal has the design to send an army and seize to-morrow, if not to-day, the kingdom of Bihar. The Lohanis for three or four descents have enjoyed *jagirs*, and live at their ease; nay, they even now covet all the newly acquired land. But I, who am your well-wisher, think it fit to entertain fresh men with the money and districts newly acquired; so that your power may be strengthened, and that when the enemy (*i.e.*, the King of Bengal) sees our large force, he may abandon his designs on the kingdom. On this account the Lohanis are dissatisfied with me, and complain of me, and are plotting to do me injury, and out of envy and hatred make all kinds of false complaints and accusations to you against me. If you believe me loyal, uphold that which I have in all loyalty done, and dissuade the Lohanis from their hostility to me, nor listen to what they say. You know that the Lohanis are a much stronger and more powerful tribe than the Surs; and the custom of the Afghans is, that if any man has four kinsmen more than another, he thinks little of killing or dishonouring his neighbour. These are troublous times: are you not anxious, and on your guard? For myself, I know the Lohanis are plotting my death. From to-day I shall come to you with every precaution. Excuse me from coming inside of the palace, or, if it be indispensable that I should go within, permit me to enter it with a strong guard."

Jalal Khan and the Lohanis perceived that Sher Khan had found them out in their designs, and that their plots had failed; so Jalal Khan said to Sher Khan, "What power have the Lohanis that they should regard you with an evil eye? All the Afghan race know that the Lohanis are a foul-mouthed people, and are without caution or prudence, and that their tongues are not under their control. They speak whatever comes to their lips, but they do not act upon it. Come to me, accompanied by your followers, in any manner that may reassure you, and permit no fear or anxiety to find a place in your mind. I will agree to whatever you do."

Thus assuring Sher Khan in every way, Jalal Khan dismissed him. But after that, the Lohanis and Sher Khan distrusted each other, and there sprang up two parties; those of the Lohanis who had given intelligence to Sher Khan sided with him, and thus the Lohanis themselves became disunited. As enmity had arisen among them, a considerable number of the Lohanis bound themselves by vows and oaths to Sher Khan, who said to them, "I cannot choose but serve Jalal Khan loyally; his father and his mother both showed me kindness; when he was very young, I was appointed to educate him, and I did not fail to use my best endeavours in his education, as he well knows." . . . . The Lohanis who had joined themselves to Sher Shah replied: "The counsel which your heart has approved is very good; for between them and ourselves there has arisen deadly enmity; it is not fitting we should be in the same place." . . . Sher Khan said to the friendly Lohanis, "The scheme which I have devised for my own protection and the good of Jalal Khan is as follows: I shall say to Jalal Khan thus: 'You have two matters in hand, one to oppose your enemy, the King of Bengal; the other, the preservation of the internal peace of the country, and the collection of revenue from the cultivators.' " . . . . The Lohanis answered: "You have now a large force with you; there is no necessity for retaining men who are seditious and ill-disposed. Say simply to Jalal Khan that he ought to send them away, and should give their *jagirs* to other soldiers." Sher Khan replied: "My object is my own safety; out of regard for one's own life, it is not good to confirm the hostility of one's enemies." . . . . All present assented, and afterwards Sher Khan wrote to Jalal Khan in the following terms: "When Sultan Muhammad exalted me to Your Majesty's deputyship, this was displeasing to the envious Lohanis. After Sultan Muhammad's death, your mother employed me in the administration of the kingdom. The envy of the Lohanis increased, and they constantly complained of me, both openly and secretly; but as my skirts were free from the contamination of dishonesty, how much soever they searched my conduct, they could find in my acts no opening through which they might effect my removal from the office of deputy. . . . The Mughals who conquered the country from Sultan Ibrahim did not do so by the sword, but through the quarrels which the Afghans had among themselves. It has become known to me from a great many sources that the Lohanis wish to assassinate me and day and night employ themselves in contriving how to get me out of the way, and presume on the greater number of their tribe. And you also have two objects; one to oppose your enemy, the ruler of Bengal; the other, to preserve the kingdom against internal enemies, and to collect the revenues. Since your army is split into two parties, opposed to each other, it is impossible to keep them both in one place; therefore, whichever of the two it pleases you keep with yourself, send the other to their *jagirs*. I have spoken because it was incumbent on me. A man's life is dear to him, he will not part with it for nothing."

When Jalal Khan was informed of this representation, he said to Sher Khan's *vakil*: "Tell Sher Khan that he has right on his side. . . . Let him wait a iittle, for I have powerful enemies; this sedition must be repressed by degrees. I will distinguish the truth from what is false." When Sher Khan was informed of the reply to his letters, he again sent his vakil to Jalal Khan's presence to say, "What Your Majesty has said is true. . . . Whatever you do, I will obey you; nor will I transgress your orders.

After this, Jalal Khan sent for the Lohanis who sought to kill Sher Khan, and showed them Sher Khan's letters, and said: "Certain of the Lohanis who were aware of your designs went to Sher Khan and informed him, and have joined themselves to him, and they have sworn and vowed, whatever good or ill betide, never to separate from each other. What is to be done?" The Lohanis who sided with Jalal Khan[17] replied: "We did not in the least care that Sher Khan has become acquainted with our designs; but it has fallen out ill that so large a number of our brethren sould have sided with him, and that disunion should have fallen on the tribe of Lohanis. . . . Do you send Sher Khan to his *jagirs,* and station him there; and do you, with a cheerful and confident mind, go to the King of Bengal, and getting a *jagir* for yourself in Bengal, make over the kingdom of Bihar to him as a present, before any one else has attempted to seize it." The advice of the Lohanis pleased Jalal Khan, who, instantly sending for Sher Khan, said: "The Lohanis, who, on account of your loyalty to me, bear enmity against you, will, please God, receive their deserts

[17] This expression would seem to imply that Jalal Khan was privy to their plot. As both private and public virtue were strangers to the hearts of these Afghan nobles, we have no reason to hesitate about the perfidy of any of them, especially as Jalal Khan was himself a Lohani. Indeed, Nia'matu-lla in both his works, distinctly says that the scheme to cut off Sher Khan was devised by the Lohanis in co-operation Jalal Khan. See Dorn, p. 96.

and punishment. Do you remain to oppose the Mughals, and also administer the affairs of the kingdom. I will go to attack the King of Bengal." Sher Khan assented, and Jalal Khan, bestowing a horse and dress of honour upon him sent him off at once.[18] When Sher Khan had reached his *jagir* at Sahsaram, Jalal Khan went over to the King of Bengal, who attached to his person a division of the army under Ibrahim Khan, son of Kutb Shah. As soon as Sher Khan heard that Jalal Khan had gone over to the King of Bengal, he was much pleased, and said: "Now the kingdom of Bihar has fallen into my hands. I felt certain that the army of the king of Bengal would assuredly come to attempt the conquest of Bihar, and as enmity existed in the army of Jalal Khan between the Lohanis and myself, I feared lest the enemy should be victorious, for the surest means of defeat are divisions in your own army. Now that the Lohanis are gone to Bengal, there are no quarrels in my army, and if there be no divisions among the Afghans, how can the Bengal Army compare with them in the day of battle? Even the Mughals cannot equal them. Please God, when I have dispersed the Bengal army, you will soon see, if I survive, how I will expel the Mughals from Hindusthan"[19] After this, Sher

[18] The object of all this is not very evident; but Nia'matu-lla says it was a sort of stratagem, by which it was devised to bring back the Bengalis as auxiliaries for the explustion of Sher Khan from Bihar. The whole counsel is worthy of the children who suggested and assented to it. See Dorn., p. 97.

[19] Nia'matu-lla tells us that one night about this time, while wandering in the bazar of Bihar,—"in which excursions he used secretly to deposit gold and clothes on the cushions of the sleeping who were oppressed by indigence,"—a *darwesh* unexpectedly raised his head and explained, "God be praised! The Emperor of Dehli has come". Which words Sher Khan regarded as a divine inspiration.—Dorn p. 98.

Khan began to strengthen himself, and enlist more men. Wherever there were any Afghans he sent to them, and gave them any money they asked. Having collected a very large force, and made every preparation, and having gained the good will of his whole army, he placed the country of Bihar in his rear, and proceeded against the army of the King of Bengal, fortifying his position with an earthen circumvallation.

The King of Bengal had appointed Ibrahim Khan the leader of his army, and despatched him to conquer the kingdom of Bihar.[20] Ibrahim Khan had under him a large Bengal army, and many elephants, and a park of artillery (*atish-bazi*). In the excess of his pride, he altogether despised the army of Sher Khan. Sher Khan, keeping under the shelter of his entrenchments, skirmished every day; and in spite of all their endeavours, the army of Ibrahim could not inflict any injury on his forces, on account of the earthen embankments. The Afghans behaved with great gallantry, and repelled the endeavours of Ibrahim Khan's army to penetrate their entrenchments. Every time the latter attacked, they were compelled to return unsuccessful; but neither army gained any solid advantage over the other. Ibrahim Khan, who was very confident in the prowess of the Bengalis, thought that in the day of battle the Afghans would be no match for them; whereas it was only from his superior numbers, his elephants, and his artillery, that he had up to that time maintained his ground against them: so he wrote to his sovereign to request reinforcements, saying that Sher Khan had taken up a fortified position, and that he was unable to dislodge him with his present force.

When Sher Khan heard that Ibrahim Khan had sent for reinforcements, he called his Afghans together and said: "I have for some time abstained from meeting the

[20] Niamatulla (*ibid*) calls him erroneously Ibrahim Shah, King of Bengal.

Bengalis in the open field, and have kept myself sheltered under entrenchments, and I have brought out only a few men to fight with them, and for this reason, lest they should be discouraged by the large numbers of the enemy. Now I am convinced that the Bengalis are much inferior to the Afghans in war. I have remained within entrenchments for some time without any general engagement, in order that the comparative prowess of the two nations might be manifested, and the presumption of the Bengalis be abated, while the Afghans might be no longer discouraged by the disparity of forces. I will now engage in open battle, for without a general engagement we cannot destroy and disperse our enemies. Praise be to God! whenever such an engagement occurs between Afghans and Bengalis, the Afghans must prevail. It is impossible that the Bengalis can stand against them. At present this is my purpose. To-morrow morning, if you concur with me, hoping in the mercy of the Protector, and trusting on this text, 'By God's command the lesser number overcomes the greater,' I will engage the enemy in open battle, for it behoves us not to delay or be backward in this matter, as reinforcements will soon reach them." The Afghans replied: "That which your noble mind has determined is extremely right." . . . .

When Sher Khan saw the Afghans were in good heart to engage the Bengalis, and that Ibrahim Khan was daily pondering how much longer Sher Khan would yet remain in his entrenchments, and was anxious for an engagement, as he so presumed on the number of his forces that he had encamped them all round Sher Khan's entrenchment, and had not thrown up any works to protect them, he determinded to give him battle; and to send his *vakil* to tell Ibrahim Khan that it behoved him to be prepared the following morning, as he intended to come out of his entrenchments for that purpose. When Shen Khan told the message to his friends, it pleased them, and he sent his *vakil* to Ibrahim Khan saying, "You have often said to me, 'Come out of your entrenchments, and let us meet in battle on the open field that we may test each other's prowess.' I have purposely remained patiently in my entrenchments for a time, hoping that peace might be concluded with you; but if you will agree to no peace, to-morrow morning put your army in array and come out, so that we may meet in open battle." Ibrahim Khan replied to the *vakil,* "Say to Sher Khan, 'Have all your forces present on the field of battle early tomorrow morning.' " When Sher Khan heard this reply, he was much delighted, and told the intelligence to his men. Ibrahim Khan also told Fath Khan to give orders that his men should be ready and present on the morrow.

When one watch of the night was yet remaining, Sher Khan arrayed his forces, and brought them out of their entrenchments; and after the morning prayers, he himself came out, and said to his chiefs, "In the enemy's army there are many elephants and guns, and a great force of infantry; we must fight them in such a manner that they shall not be able to preserve their original order." The Bengali cavalry should be drawn away from their guns and infantry, and the horses intermingled with the elephants, so that their array may be disordered. I have thought of a stratagem by which to defeat the Bengalis. I will draw up the greater part of my forces behind the cover of that height which we see, but will retain for the attack a small number of experienced and veteran horse. Now, they will fight exactly in the same manner as they did on the former occasion, without any expectation of defeat. I will bring up my selected division, who, after discharging one flight of arrows into the Bengali army, shall retreat. Ibrahim Khan still bears in mind the old feud regarding the death of his father, and is presumptuous on account of his superior force. He will think the Afghans are beginning to fly; and, becoming eager, he will leave his artillery and foot on the rear, and press on with all expedition himself, and disorder and confusion will find their way into his order of battle. I will then bring out my force which had been concealed behind the eminence, who will attack the enemy. The Bengali cavalry, deprived of the support of their artillery and infantry, are by themselves unable to cope with the Afghan horse. I hope, by the favour of God, that their force will be routed and put to flight." All the Afghans expressed their approbation of Sher Khan's plan of battle, and were much delighted, and observed there could be no better possible scheme devised.

After this was agreed upon, Sher Khan drew out, as described above, a picked force, and explained to them that they were to act as had been determined; and the rest of his force he drew up behind the shelter of the rising ground. When the army of Ibrahim Khan was descried, the horsemen, according to their instructions, coming up to the Bengali army, discharged one volley of arrows, and then turned about. The Bengali cavalry, supposing the Afghans were flying, broke their ranks, just as Sher Khan had anticipated, and perused the Afghans. Accordingly, as soon as Sher Khan perceived that the Bengali cavalry had advanced, and left their infantry and artillery in the rear, he appeared at the head of his force which had been lying in ambuscade, and advanced. The Bengalis were panic-struck, and the Afghans, who had fled returned, and, joining the rest, they all stirrup to stirrup, after the manner of the Afghans, fell upon the hostile army. The Bengalis, however, rallied, and stood their ground, and the two armies became closely engaged. After warriors of note had fallen in the contest, the sun of victory rose in favour of Sher Khan from the horizon of the East, and the Bengali army was defeated. Ibrahim Khan exerted himself much, and said to the Bengalis, "Turn and exert yourselves for the army of the Afghans is small. What face can we show to the king?" But it was no use. . . . Ibrahim Khan again said to his men; "What face can I show to the king?" . . . . I will either be victorious or die." He exerted himself much; but as his (term of) life had arrived, he was killed.

Jalal Khan fled to the King of Bengal. The whole of the treasure, elephants, and train of artillery (*top-khana*) fell into the hands of Sher Khan, who was thus supplied with munitions of war, and became master of the kingdom of Bihar, and of much other territory besides. Since God, the most holy and omnipotent, had pre-ordained from all eternity to give the kingdom of Hind to Sher Khan, and that the people of the Lord should live in ease and comfort under the shadow of his justice and that he should be a zealous and just ruler, his wealth daily increased, and the whole country gradually came into his possession. He employed himself in the improvement of his provinces, so that, in a short time, they much surpassed their previous condition, and reached to perfection;—for this reason, that he personally superintended every business; nor did he show favour to any oppressor, even though of his own relations or dependants; and if any one entered his service, he said to him from the first; "The stipend and maintenance which I may agree to give you, I will pay you in full, and not diminish them a single *falus;* but you shall not oppress or quarrel with any one. If you do, I will visit you with such a punishment as shall be an example to others." In a short season he acquired a good reputation among the people of God, and it was everywhere known that Sher Khan paid his troops regularly, and neither oppressed any one himself, nor suffered others to do so.

I, the author of this history of Sher Khan, 'Abbas Khan bin Shaikh Ali Sarwani, have heard from my kindred and connexions, who were great nobles and companions of Sher Khan, that he got possession of the fort of Chunar in the following manner. Sultan Ibrahim Lodi had entrusted the fort of Chunar to Taj Khan Sarangkhani, and the royal treasures were deposited in the fort. Now this Taj Khan was altogether a slave to his love for his wife Lad Malika, who was a woman of great sagacity and wisdom; and Taj Khan had made three Turkoman brothers his lieutenants, by name Mir Ahmad, Is'hak, and Mir Dad; they were own brothers, experienced, talented, and wise men. As they perceived that Taj Khan was completely under the control of his wife, they of course ingratiated themselves with her, and promised and swore to Lad Malika that they would not oppose her, and would be faithful to her.

Lad Malika had no sons, but Taj Khan had several sons by other wives. On account of his affection for Lad Malika, he did not give a fitting maintenance to his sons, and their mothers did not even receive a sufficiency of daily food. Although the sons often reconstrated, it was of no avail. Hence they continually laid up the seeds of enmity and hate against Lad Malika. One night Taj Khan's eldest son wounded Lad Malika with a sabre, but not severely. Her servants complained to Taj Khan, who drew his sword, and ran out to kill his son. He perceiving that his father was about to kill him for the sake of his wife, struck his father with his sabre, and escaped out of the house. Taj Khan died of the wound.

The sons of Taj Khan, although but young, were on bad terms with the greater part of his troops; but Lad Malika being a clever woman, by the liberality and benevolence of her conduct, had ingratiated herself with them during Taj Khan's lifetime, and after his death also they adhered to her. A few ill-disposed persons adhered to Taj Khan's sons; but they daily quarrelled, and disputed among themselves over the treasure, and showed themselves so incapable, that their followers became disgusted with them. Sher Khan therefore sent secretly to Mir Ahmad, saying, "Send Mir Dad to me, for I have a message for you which I will send through him." Mir Ahmad sent Mir Dad to Sher Khan, who said to him, "Tell Mir Ahmad that I am ready to confer great benefits on him." Mir Ahmad when he heard this, said to his brothers, "Lad Malika possesses talent for government, yet she is but a woman; and there are many who covet the fort and the treasure in it. Lad Malika will not be able to hold the fort, therefore it is best that I should surrender the fort to Sher Khan, and so lay him under an obligation to myself; it will be to our advantage." The brothers approved of Mir Ahmad's counsel, and went to Lad Malika, and showing to her Sher Khan's letters, said, "We obey you, whatever you order us that we will do." She replied, "You are to me as father and brothers; do what you like, I will agree to whatever you say." They said. "If you will not be angry we will say what we consider to be most to your advantage." She replied, "Fear not; speak without hesitation the purpose you entertain." Mir Ahmad said, "Even if there should be no disturbance in the fort, still you would be unable to hold it, for you are a woman and have no sons, and there are many persons who seek to gain possession of it. It is a royal possession, and until some one assumes the sovereignty, it will be best to give the fort over to Sher Khan. You shall marry him, and thus find an asylum, and so no one shall deprive you of the fort and royal treasures." Lad Malika said, "Send your brother Mir Dad to Sher Khan in order to arrange with him that I shall give up the fort; but on one condition, that he shall deprive of his ears and nose that miserable sons who murdered his father, that he may be a warning to others."

When Mir Dad came to Sher Khan, he made him agree that he would not hurt or injure Lad Malika or the mother of the three brothers, Sher Khan received him with all honour and hospitality, and using every endeavour to assure him, and making the utmost protestations of friendship and good feeling, said, "If Lad Mailka gives me up the fort and will marry me, I shall be for ever indebted to your kindness." And Sher Khan thus having employed himself in captivating the bud of his heart by kindness, Mir Dad said, "It is not fit to surrender the fort except to the king; but since I have come to you, you have shown me such kindness and goodwill, and have displayed such hospitality, that I have considered nothing but how, in return for this, to get the fort into your power. I will not fail to use my best exertions to this end. My hope in God is, that Lad Malika will not dissent from what I say; but when the business is performed to your heart's content, do not so act as to disgrace me." Sher Khan swearing everything he wished, assured him and said, "While I live I will never cause you grief. . . . Mir Dad recommended that they should start at once and Sher Khan mounting with all haste set off. Mir Dad went on before and gave intelligence that Sher Khan was coming, and urged them not to delay giving up the fort, and got Lad Malika and his brothers to consent. So Mir Dad was sent back to bring in Sher Khan quickly, and to take possession of the fort before the sons of Taj Khan should be aware of their designs.

As soon as Mir Dad had come to Sher Khan, and had told him that it was agreed to give him up the fort and treasure, and that he should marry Lad Malika, and when he had admitted him at once into the fort, they immediately proceeded to celebrate the marriage between Lad Malika and Sher Khan. She gave him a present consisting of 150 of the most exceedingly valuable jewels, and seven *mans* of pearls, and 150 *mans* of gold, and many other articles and ornaments.[21] Sher Khan subsequently got into his power and possession the *parganas* near the fort of Chunar; and after this, he strengthened his resources still further by inheriting sixty *mans* of gold from Guhar Kusain, widow of Nasir Khan.[22] His power was

[21] Ahmad Yadgar gives a different enumeration (MS., p. 262), but gives the total value at nine lacs of rupees.

[22] Dr. Dorn, *History of the Afghans*, p. 101 says, "600 *mans* of pure gold, besides many other rarities of

now firmly established, as he was master of a fort and of much of the treasure of the kingdom, and had collected a large force, both horse and foot. After this Sultan Mahmud, the son of Sultan Sikandar, whom Hasan Khan Mewatti and the Rana Sanga,[23] and certain Afghans had set up as king, engaged the second Jamshid the Emperor Babar in an action near Sikri, in which Hasan Khan, son of Adil Khan Mewatti, and the Raja of Dungarpur, Rawal by name, were slain, and Sultan Mahmud and the Rana Sanga being defeated fled to Chitor. Sultan Mahmud remained for a season in that neighbourhood, and afterwards came towards Patna. Masnad Ali Azam Khan Humayun Sani (whose son-in-law Sultan Mahmud was), Masnad Ali Isa Khan, son of Haibat Khan, the son of Mansad Ali Umar Khan Kalkapuria,[24] who had formerly been governor of Lahore, and Ibrahim Khan, son of Ahmad Khan, son of Mubariz Khan Yusuf-Khail, and Mian Babin, son of Mian Atta Sahu-khail, governor of Sirhind, and Mian Bayazid Farmuli, had at that time assembled themselves together and threw obstacles in the way of the Mughals. Mian Babin and Mian Bayazid were the leaders of a large force, and had very often fought against the Mughals, and had obtained a great name for their valour. These nobles invited Sultan Mahmud to Patna, and made him king. When Sultan Mahmud came with these nobles unto Bihar, Sher Khan found it impossible to offer any resistance, as he possessed

various descriptions." This is not borne out by the Persian originals, which all read only "sixty," instead of "600." [Gen. Cunningham's MS. agrees with the translation. Literally it says, "Afterwards Guhar Kushain, the wife (widow) of Nasir Khan, died, and sixty *mans* of her gold came into the hands of Sher Shah." But Sir H. Elliot's MS. says, "After this he married Guhar Kushain, the widow, and sixty *mans* etc., etc.

[23] The "Rana Sanka" of Babar's Memoirs.

[24] Var. Kaktur.

so considerable a force, and he himself was not held in sufficient repute among the Afghans to admit of such an attempt. He was therefore necessitated to present himself before Sultan Mahmud. The Afghans portioned out among themselves the kingdom of Bihar,[25] but the king said to him, "When I get possession of Jaunpur, I will give to you the kingdom of Bihar which you conquered after defeating the army of the King of Bengal. Be not at all uneasy, as Sultan Sikandar bestowed the kingdom of Bihar upon Darya Khan, so will I bestow it on you." Sher Khan requested a *farman* to this effect, and Sultan Mahmud assented, and ordered one to be executed, and so Sher Khan received a *farman* for the kingdom of Bihar from the king; and having taken several months' leave, returned to his *jagir* to prepare his forces.

When Sultan Mahmud had equipped his army, he marched towards Jaunpur, and issued a mandate directing Sher Khan to join him immediately. On the receipt of this order, Sher Khan wrote back in reply, that he would come as soon as he could complete the arrangement about his force. When the nobles about the king knew the purport of Sher Khan's reply, they represented that Sher Khan was in confederacy with the Mughals, and was merely finessing and making pretences, and that the king ought not to trust what he wrote or said, but to compel him to accompany the army. 'Azam Humayun Sarwani said: "It will be easy to bring Sher Khan along with us. Put your mind at ease. Let us march in the direction of his *jagir*, and go wherever Sher Khan may be. As punishment for his delay, let us exact from him a large and handsome reception, and then let us compel him to join us." Sultan Mahmud and his nobles were greatly pleased at 'Azam Humayun's advice, and praised his sagacity. They proceeded by regular marches to

[25] Nia'matu-lla adds, "except Sahsaram, which was the old *jagir* of Sher Khan."—Dorn., p. 101.

Sahsaram, where Sher Khan then was. Sher Khan hearing that Sultan Mahmud was come with all his followers, and would compel him to join them, whether he would or no, was much vexed and said to his friends, "The plan I had devised has not succeeded. Of the nobles who are with the king, two—the one named Azam Humayun, and the other Isa Khan Sarwani—are cleaver and wise men, and have much experience in public affairs. They have joined this army for the honour of the Afghans and from regard to their kindred; albeit, they are aware that the army will do no good, for the nobles who are in it are not at unity among themselves, and without unity they can accomplish nothing. . . . . I can no longer excuse myself, I must go along with the army. Do you tell your troops to prepare for marching with all haste, while I go out to meet the king and his army myself, and put them in good humour, make my own excuses, and bring them with me; for my guests are my own kin, and do you make all preparations for entertaining them." Sher Khan then went out to welcome the king, and having prepared rich entertainments of divers kinds, sent them to the quarters of the various nobles and chiefs, who were his friends, according to their rank; and also gave large presents and a magnificent entertainment to Sultan Mahmud, so that all parties were pleased and delighted with him.

Sher Khan requested Sultan Mahmud to halt a few days, while he equipped his forces. Sultan Mahmud acceded to this request, and after a halt of some days, Sher Khan having made his preparations, marched in company with Sultan Mahmud. When they approached Jaunpur, the Mughals who were there abandoned the place and fled. Sultan Mahmud delayed some days at Jaunpur, but sent on his army in advance and occupied Lucknow and other districts.

On hearing this intelligence, the Emperor Humayun

set off from Agra[26] for Lucknow, whither Sultan Mahmud arrived also from Jaunpur. The two armies met near Lucknow, and daily skirmishes ensued. Warriors on either side came out and engaged one another. Sher Khan perceiving that there was no unanimity among the Afghans, but that every one acted as he thought best, wrote to Hindu Beg, and said, "The Mughals raised me from the dust. These people have brought me with them by force; but in the day of battle I will not fight, and will go off the field without engaging. Tell the Emperor Humayun the true state of my case, and that I will serve him in the day of battle, and will cause the defeat of this army." When Hindu Beg showed Sher Khan's letter to the Emperor, the latter ordered him to write to Sher Khan, "Be at your ease as to your accompanying these people; act as you have written; if you do, it will be for your advancement." After some days had elapsed, the two armies joined in a general engagement, and Sher Khan drew off his forces at the critical moment of the battle and retreated without engaging. This caused Sultan Mahmud's defeat. Ibrahim Khan Yusuf-Khail made desperate exertions, and showed great gallantry in that engagement, nor did he quit his post while life remained; he repulsed every Mughal force which was opposed to him; but was at last slain. As Mian Bayazid had drunk more wine than he could bear, and had got drunk and careless, he also was slain in that battle. Sultan Mahmud and the other chiefs being defeated, fled to the kingdom of Bihar. The Sultan had

[26] I concur with Elphinstone (*History of India*, vol. ii, 128), in considering this march to have commenced in Safar, 944 H. (July, 1537 A.D.) He says the *Tarikh-i Sher Shahi* says 942. Which one? Not this. Firishta and Khaki Shirazi say 943; but there is impossibility in the former date, and great improbability in the latter. All the Afghan histories of the period are very deficient and contradictory in their dates.

neither money nor territory to entertain a force of his own, and his nobles who had placed him on the throne were most of them killed in the battle at Lucknow, while the few who remained were from their quarrels dispersed. Sultan Mahmud was greatly given to dancing women, and passed most of his time in amusing himself; as he had no power to oppose the Mughals, he abdicated his royalty, and went and settled himself in the province of Patna, and never again attempted the throne. He died in A. H. 949.[27]

When Humayun had overcome Sultan Mahmud, and had put the greater number of his opponents to death, he sent Hindu Beg to take Chunar from Sher Khan, but Sher Khan declined to give it up to him. When he heard this, Humayun commanded his victorious standards to be set in motion towards Chunar. Sher Khan leaving Jalal Khan (who after the death of Sher Khan succeeded him under the title of Islam Shah), and another Jalal Khan, son of Jalu, in Chunar, withdrew with his family and followers to the hills of Nahrkunda.[28] The army of Humayun besieged Chunar, and daily fighting ensued, in which both Jalal Khans displayed valour great beyond description, and from their gallantry gained great renown. Sher Khan's custom was to despatch spies to all the neighbouring countries, in order to inquire into their actual condition.

Sher Khan knew that the Emperor Humayun would be unable to delay long in those parts; for his spies brought him word that Bahadur Shah, the King of Gujarat had conquered the kingdom of Mandu, and was meditating the seizure of Dehli, and would shortly declare war. Humayun also having received this intelli-

[27] The *Tarikh-i Khan Jahan* (MS.. p. 165) says that he died in Orissa in 944 H. The *Tarikh-i-Daudi* (MS. p. 211) says in Orissa in 949 H.

[28] [Var. "Bahrkunda"]

gence, Sher Khan sent his *vakil* to him and wrote saying: "I am your slave. and the client of Junaid Birlas. Moreover, the good service which I did at the battle of Lucknow is known to you, and as you must entrust the fort of Chunar to some one, make it over to me, and I will send my son Kutb Khan to accompany you in this expedition. Do you lay aside all anxiety as regards these parts; for if either I or any other Afghans do any act unbefitting or disloyal, you have my son with you; inflict on him such reprisals as may be a warning to others."

When Sher Khan's emissary represented this to the Emperor Humayun, he replied: "I will give Chunar to Sher Khan, but on this condition, that he sends Jalal Khan with me." Sher Khan sent word in reply, "In the love and estimation of their father and mother, all sons are alike. Jalal Khan is not superior to Kutb Khan, but I have many opponents and I have vowed that I will not permit one to get a footing in the country, lest afterwards the Emperor should be compelled to war with him." Just at this time news arrived that Mirza Muhammad Zaman,[29] who had been sentenced to imprisonment in the fort of Bayana, had regained his liberty by producing a forged *farman* for his release, and had created a disturbance in the country; and also that Bahadur Shah of Gujarat was intending to march on Dehli. So Humayun said to Sher Khan's agent, that as Sher Khan was a loyal man, he would agree to this proposal, and that if he would send Kutb Khan, he would leave the fort of Chunar with Sher Khan. Sher Khan was delighted and sent Kutb Khan his son and Isa Khan

[29] He was grandson of Sultan Hussain Mirza, and endeavoured to supplant Humayun on the throne of India by two different schemes of assassination. After various other treacheries and machinations, he was again reconciled to Humayun, and was killed at the battle of Chaunsa in 946 H., which was lost chiefly through his supineness and neglect.

his chamberlain, to the Emperor, who set off for Agra, and employed himself in suppressing the rebellion of Sultan Bahadur.[30] Sher Khan took advantage of this opportunity, and did not leave one enemy of his remaining throughout the kingdom of Bihar. He also began to patronize all Afghans. Many of them, who had assumed the garb of religious mendicants on account of their misfortunes, he relieved, and enlisted as soldiers: and some who refused to enlist, and preferred a life of mendicancy, he put to death, and declared he would kill every Afghan who refused to be a soldier. He was also very careful of his Afghans in action, that their lives might not be uselessly sacrificed. When the Afghans heard that Sher Khan was eagerly desirous of patronizing their race, they entered into his service from all directions.

Sultan Bahadur being defeated, went towards Surat, and the whole of the Afghans who were in his service, whether chiefs or common soldiers, came to Sher Khan. Several powerful chiefs, who had at first scorned to enter Sher Khan's service, when they saw his power day by day increasing, put aside their pride, and volunteered to serve under him. Accordingly 'Azam Humayun Sarwani and Masnad Ali 'Isa Khan son of Masnad Ali Haibat Khan Sahu-khail, and Mian Babin Sahu-khail, Kutb Khan Mochi-khail, Maruf Farmuli, and Azam Humayun, eldest son of Sultan Alam Khan Sahu-khail, and in short every Afghan of high rank joined him and he assumed the title of Hazrat Ali.

Bibi Fath Malika exceedingly wealthy; she was the daughter of Mian Kala Pahar[31] Farmuli, sister's son to

[30] Nearly all the other authorities inform us that Kutb Khan effected his escape from Humayun's camp. Ahmad Yadgar (MS. p. 264) says that he succeeded in doing this at Ajmir.

[31] [Or "Bihar."]

Sultan Bahlol. This Mian Muhammad was a very prudent man; he entertained but few soldiers, and gave his chief attention to the accumulation of wealth. Sultan Bahlol gave him in *jagir* the whole of *sarkar* of Oudh, and several *parganas* besides. He inherited also wealth from his father. During the reigns of Sultans Bahlol, Sikandar, and Ibrahim, his *jagirs* were never disturbed, and during all this time he gave his attention to nothing else except the accumulation of wealth. I have heard from persons of veracity that he had amassed three hundred *mans* of red hard[32] gold, and he did not purchase any other but golden jewelry. He had no child save Fath Malika, and he married her to a lad named Shaikh Mustafa.

When Mian Muhammad died, towards the end of the reign of Sultan Ibrahim, he left one boy of uncertain parentage, who was called Mian Nia'mu. His parentage was for this cause uncertain as Mian Kala Pahar had bestowed one of his concubines on a servant. When the girl had been some time in the servant's house, she bore a male child, whom she declared to be the offspring of Mian Muhammad Kala Pahar. When Mian Muhammad heard this, he took the girl away from his servant, and brought her into his own house, and acknowledged the child as his own son. The child grew up an able man. Sultan Ibrahim made Shaikh Mustafa, the husband of Fath Malika, and who was also her father's brother's son, the successor to Mian Muhammad Kala Pahar; but gave a small portion of Kala Pahar's treasury to Mian Nia'mu, and also bestowed one or two *parganas* of the *sarkar* of Oudh in *jagir* on him; but the greater portion of Kala Pahar's treasure came into the possession of Fath Malika.

This Mustafa, during the time of Sultan Ibrahim

[32] This word appears variously, "*hashi*", "*jashi*", and "*chasi*".

and afterwards, distinguished himself in action.[33] I have heard from various relators of history, that during the lifetime of Sultan Ibrahim, Mian Mustafa and Mian Ma'ruf Farmuli quarrelled regarding some territory, and fought about it. It was Mian Mustafa's custom, when about to engage, to prepare sundry *mans* of sweetmeats in commemoration of his father Mian Muhammad, and distribute them to *fakirs*. This done, he used to set off to fight. Mian Ma'ruf employed himself in reading prayers and supplications.

When Mian Mustafa died, he left a young daughter, by name Mihr Sultan. Fath Malika, being a very able woman, had educated Mian Bayazid, a younger brother of Mustafa. She said to him, "Do you look to the soldiery, I will provide money." Mian Bayazid with this money collected a very large force, and greatly distinguished himself, gaining several victories over the troops of the Emperor Babar; so that the names of Mian Babin and Mian Bayazid became famous; but since the death of Bayazid has been already described, there is no need for repeating the story here. When he was slain, Fath Malika was in Bihar, and collecting a number of men to protect the treasure, she proceeded to the hills adjoining Bihar. intending to go. to Patna; for the Raja of Patna had shown great favour to the more wealthy Afghans. When Bayazid was killed and Sultan Mahmud had given up striving for the Empire, the Raja of Patna considered that the fortune of the Afghan connexion was on the decline, and stretched out the hand of oppression against the possessions of the Afghans to whom he had given shelter. Fath Malika, on hearing this news, abandoned her intention of going to Patna. When Sher Khan heard that the Bibi, from this apprehension, had abandoned her design of going to Patna, he was much delighted and conceived the intention of getting Fath Malika,

[33] He will be found mentioned under that reign.

by means of some pretence or stratagem, into his own clutches, lest she should go into the territories of some other potentate, and the treasure should thus slip out of his grasp, which would have grieved him to all eternity. So he sent his *vakil* to the Bibi, and wrote to this effect: "The nobles and grandees of Sultans Bahlol and Sikandar have come into these parts, and have honoured me by taking shelter with me, and are collected together for the honour of the Afghans. Your servant also has girt up his loins in this cause and design, and you have strong claims on the consideration of the Afghan race, first because you are of the family of Shaikh Muhammad; secondly there is your connexion with a descendant of Sultan Bahlol. What fault has your servant committed, that you delay in visting his country? There is no trusting the promises of the unbelievers of these parts; and (which God forbid!) if any injury should occur to your people among these hills in which you now are, it would be an eternal disgrace to me. Men would say, 'Because she could not trust Sher Khan, she would not enter his country.' " When the *vakil* came to Fath Malika, and she heard what Sher Khan wrote, she wrore in reply, that if he would make a covenant with her and confirm it by oaths, she would come to him. To this Sher Khan agreed, and she sent a trustworthy man to Sher Khan, in whose presence he swore, and pledged himself by the most solemn oaths. Bibi Fath Malika being fully assured, came to Sher Khan, and remained some time with him.

When Nasib Shah, the ruler of Bengal, died, the nobles of Bengal made Sultan Mahmud his successor; but he was not able to manage the kingdom, and it fell into disorder. Sher Khan conceived the desire of seizing the kingdom of Bengal, and took from the Bibi 300 *mans* of gold to equip his army; and gave her two *parganas* for her support (*madad-ma'ash*), besides leaving her some ready money for her immediate expenses.[34] But Jalal Khan having, against the Bibi's consent, wished to espouse her daughter Mihr Sultan, Sher Khan, on hearing of it, forbade Jalal Khan; and she married her daughter to one Sultan Sikandar, a relation of her own. This Sikandar proved very unworthy. During Mihr Sultan's life he lived in comfort; and in the reign of the Emperor Akbar, in the year 975 A. H. Mihr Ṣultan, on her way to the *parganas* of Kayat, in the direction of Sind, died in the house of Muzaffar Khan. Sher Khan having equipped his army with this money, attacked the kingdom of Bengal, and got possession of all of it on this side Ghari (Sikri-gali).

When the Emperor Humayun came back from Gujarat, the Khan-khanan Yusuf-khail (who brought the Emperor Babar from Kabul to Hindustan) said to him: "It is not wise to neglect Sher Khan, for he is rebelliously inclined, and well understands all matters pertaining to government; moreover, all the Afghans are collected round him." The Emperor Humayun, relying on the vastness of his forces, and on the pride of Empire, took no heed of Sher Khan, and remaining the rainy season at

[34] Dr. Dorn (p. 105) says she had placed her "district under the protection of the Mughals. At this Sher Khan was so enraged, that he seized upon her whole wealth and effects. . . . This treasure is said to have consisted of 600 *mans* of pure gold, besides specie and other valuables." This is not at all in accordance with any original MS. I have seen, which simply says: "Having escaped the violence of the Mughals, she sought refuge in this kingdom. . . . They say, that amongst her property were sixty *mans* of red gold besides silver and valuables". Here the deliberate treachery of this belauded king is not attempted to be accounted for, as it is in Dr. Dorn's translation. The *Tarikh-i Khan Jahan* (MS. p. 174) has 300 *mans*.

Agra, sent Hindu Beg to Jaunpur, with directions to write a full and true report regarding Sher Khan.

When Sher Khan heard that the Emperor Humayun intended himself marching towards Bihar, he sent magnificent presents to Hindu Beg, governor of Jaunpur, and gained his goodwill. At the same time Sher Khan wrote thus: "From what I promised I have not departed. I have not invaded the Emperor's country. Kindly write to the Emperor; and assuring him of my loyalty, dissuade him from marching in this direction; for I am his servant and well-wisher." When Hindu beheld Sher Khan's presents, he approved of them, and was well pleased, and he said to the *vakil,* "So long as I live, let your mind be easy. No one shall injure you." And in the presence of Sher Khan's *vakil,* Hindu Beg wrote a letter to the Emperor Humayun, saying: "Sher Khan is a loyal servant of Your Majesty, and strikes coin and reads the *khutba* in your name, and has not transgressed the boundaries of Your Majesty's territory, or done anything since your departure which could be any cause of annoyance to you." The Emperor, on receipt of Hindu Beg's letter, deferred his journey that year. Sher Khan, meanwhile, detached Jalal Khan, Khawas Khan senior, and other chiefs, to conquer Bengal and the city of Gaur. On their entering Bengal, Sultan Mahmud, unable to oppose them, retired to the fort of Gaur. The Afghans having made themselves masters of the surrounding country, invested and besieged that fortress, before which daily skirmishes took place.

The following year the Emperor marched towards Bihar and Bengal. When he arrived near Chunar, he consulted his nobles whether he should first take Chunar, or march towards Gaur, which the son of Sher Khan was besieging, but had not yet taken. All his Mughal nobles advised that he should first take Chunar, and then march on Gaur, and it was so determined; but when Humayun asked the Khan-khanan Yusuf-Khail for his opinion, he (having previously heard that the Mughal nobles had agreed it was advisable first to take Chunar) said, "It is a counsel of the young to take Chunar first; the counsel of the aged is, that as there is much treasure in Gaur, it is advisable to take Gaur first; after that the capture of Chunar is an easy matter." The Emperor replied: "I am young and prefer the counsel of the young. I will not leave the fort of Chunar in my rear." The author has heard from the Khan-khanan's companions, that when he returned to his quarters, he observed: "The luck of Sher Khan is great, that the Mughals do not go to Gaur. Before they take this fort, the Afghans will have conquered Gaur, and all its treasures will fall into their hands."

Sher Khan left Ghazi Sur and Bulaki,[35] who was the commandant of Chunar, in that fortress, and removed his family and those of his Afghan followers to the fortress of Bahrkunda; but as he had many families with him, that fort could not hold them all. There existed a friendly connexion between Sher Khan and the Raja of the fort of Rohtas, and Churaman, the Raja's *naib*, was on particular terms of intimate friendship and alliance with Sher Khan. This Churaman was a Brahman, and was a person of the highest rank, and had formerly shown kindness to the family of Mian Nizam, own brother to Sher Khan, and procured them shelter in the fort of Rohtas; and when all danger had gone by, the family again quitted the fort, and made it over to the Raja. On the present occasion, Sher Khan wrote that he was in great straits, and that if the Raja would give him the loan of the fort for a short time, he would be obliged to him all his days, and that when all danger was past he would again restore the fort. Churaman replied, "Be of good cheer, I will manage it, so that the Raja shall lend

[35] In other MSS., "Sultan Sarwani," and "Sultan Baroli."

you the fort." When Churaman went to the Raja, he said, "Sher Khan has asked for the loan of Rohtas for his family. He is your neighbour. This is my advice, it is an opportunity to show kindness; you should admit his family". The Raja agreed.

When Sher Khan sent his family from Bahrkunda, the Raja retracted his promise, and said, "When I admitted Mian Nizam into the fort, they had but a small force. I was the stronger. Now they have the larger force, and I a small one. If I admit them into the fort, and they will not restore it, I cannot take it from them by force." Churaman wrote to Sher Khan, saying: "Certain persons, my enemies, have given very evil counsel to the Raja, and persuaded him to violate his promise and to decline giving you the fort." Sher Khan, on receiving this news was much grieved and anxious, and he wrote to the Raja, and said: "On the faith of your promise, I have brought my family from Bahrkunda. If the Emperor Humayun hears this news, he will send his army, and all the families of the Afghans will be taken and enslaved. This misfortune will rest on your head." Sher Khan also gave to Churaman a bribe of six *mans* of gold and said: "Persuade in any way you can the Raja to give me the loan of this fort for a few days, for my family; but if he will not give it, then I will go and make my peace with the Emperor Humayun, and will revenge myself on everything belonging to the Raja." Churaman said, "Be of good heart, I will procure admittance for your women and children." So Churaman then went to the Raja, and said: "It is not becoming your dignity to break your promise. Sher Khan, on the strength of it, has brought his family from the fort of Bahrkunda. If the Emperor hears that his family is not in safety, he will attack and destroy them, and the blame will rest on my shoulders. Moreover if Sher Khan be in extremities, he will make peace with the Emperor, and will attack you, and you are not strong enough to oppose him. Why do you thus heedlessly provoke his hostility, and throw your kingdom into confusion? I am a Brahman, and since Sher Khan came here relying on my word, if his family be slain, the blame will rest on me. If you do not admit him into the fort, I will take poison and die at your door." When the Raja saw Churaman thus determined, he agreed to admit the family of Sher Khan into the fort. Sher Khan had not heard of the permission, when he received intelligence that Khawas Khan senior had been drowned in the ditch of the fort of Gaur, and that the fort of Chunar had surrendered to the Emperor Humayun.[36] He became very depressed and anxious, and bestowing on the younger brother of Khawas Khan, whose name was Musahib Khan, the surname of Khawas Khan, detached him with urgent instructions, that since Chunar had fallen, and that the Emperor Humayun would in a few days march towards Bengal, he was to press the siege of Gaur with all possible despatch.

Khawas Khan arrived at Gaur, and said to Jalal Khan, "My orders from the king[37] are to take the fort of Gaur without delay, as the Emperor is coming up in our rear." Jalal Khan said: "Wait yet to-day." But Khawas Khan replied, "I cannot disobey my orders; we must at once make the attack." Jalal Khan said: "Be it so! go to your post." Khawas Khan, taking his leave of Jalal Khan, came to his brother's post, and encouraged his brother's force saying, "My orders are these: The

[36] Respecting the capture of Chunar, and the cruelties, perpetrated on the garrison by the Mughals, see the history of Humayun. It is passed over very cursorily by all the Afghan writers, while the Timurians expatiate upon it. Elphinstone's date of 15th Shaban, 944 (8th January, 1538), for the commencement of the siege, is the most probable one.

[37] This title is now first applied to Sher Khan in the MSS.

instant I arrive to use every endeavour to take the fort and not in any way to delay." He directed the heralds to command the army to prepare themselves with all haste as there was no time to lose; and arming himself, he sent to Jalal Khan to say, "I am ready with my whole force in obedience to the orders of Sher Khan, and only wait for you. Do you array yourselves also; it is not good to delay. By God's grace we will be victorious." Jalal Khan, Shuja'at Khan, and the rest were displeased, but nevertheless, got ready. Khawas Khan personally displayed such energy and gallantry, that he succeeded in mastering the fortress even before Jalal Khan arrived. From that day his valour became celebrated, and after that he conquered wherever he went so that in all Sher Khan's army there was none like him for intrepidity as well as liberality.

Gaur having fallen, Jalal Khan sent an account of the victory to his father, and attributed it to Khawas Khan. On hearing the news, Sher Khan was exceedingly delighted; and Churaman also came to him, and said that the Raja had consented to give him the fort of Rohtas, into which he might bring his women and children. Sher Khan brought his women and children near to the fort, and expressed his devoted friendship for and obligation to the Raja, and gave him much money and goods of various kinds, saying: "If ever I am again prosperous, I will not consider myself absolved from my obligations to you". The Raja was much delighted, and said, "The fort of Rohtas is yours, order in your family." Sher Khan had given orders to his men that none should go out who once went in; after this, Sher Khan himself went in and examined the fort. He thanked God, and said: "The fort of Chunar is no fort in comparison with this; as that has gone out of my possession, this has come into it. I was not so pleased at the conquest of Gaur, as (I am) at getting possession of Rohtas." And he said to the guards of the fort, "You had best go to the Raja, and say, 'You cannot remain in the same place with the Afghans, or it will be the worse for you!'" And he ordered his own men, if the guards did not obey the order to leave the fort, to eject them by force. Sher Khan's men were all prepared, as, when they told the guards what Sher Khan had said, and these refused, they turned them out by force of arms. So Sher Khan placed his own guards and sentries in every part of the fort, and took the greatest precaution for its safe custody, and drove the Raja away from the fort. In the manner thus described he got possession of the fort of Rohtas.

The commonly received report that Sher Khan put Afghans into *dolis,* and sent them into the fort as women, is altogether erroneous and false.[38] For I, the

[38] Our author is strictly followed by the *Makhzan-i Afghani;* but the *Tarikh-i Khan-Jahan* adheres to the *doli* story. It says (MS. p. 168) that there were 1200 litters, in each of which were two Afghans armed, except in some of the foremost, in which there were old women. After the examination of some of the leading litters, Sher Khan sent a message to the Raja, to represent that the Raja having now satisfied himself there were only women in the litters, and as it was highly indecorous to expose them to the gaze of the sentries, the search ought to be discontinued. The Raja readily assented, and when the litters had all been introduced, and discharged their burdens, the Afghans seized possession of the gates, and admitted Sher Shah who was ready with his army outside, awaiting the successful result of his stratagem. Ahmad Yadgar (MS. p. 266) says that there were 300 litters, with two soldiers in each, and four Rohillas as bearers, that they killed the Raja, and then made a general massacre of the garrison. Firishta also accredits (vol. ii. p. 115) the *doli* story, and calls the Raja, Hari Krishn Rai, and says he escaped with a few followers by a private passage. By the Timurian authors the seizure of Rohtas by treachery is spoken of with an indignation

writer of this history, *Tuhfa-i Akbar Shahi,* the son of Shaikh Ali, have inquired of several chiefs and nobles who were with Sher Khan in the affair. For example, I inquired of the chief of great nobles Muzaffar Khan, and nephew of Masnad Ali Isa Khan, and of Shaikh Muhammad, son of Mian Bayazid Sarwani, and several others who were present on the occasion; and they said, "It is needful you should hear from us the history of your ancestors, for you are connected with Sultan Bahlol, Sultan Sikandar, Sher Shah, and Salim Shah. Take heed to our words, for after a lapse of many days, frequent errors and mistakes arise. We will tell you what we heard and saw." I said to Khan-'azam Muzaffar Khan, son of Jalal Khan, the son of Haibat Khan, "It is commonly said that Sher Khan took Rohtas by introducing the Afghans in covered litters, and you contradict this story. I do not know whom to believe. He replied: "You know I was with the followers of Masnad Ali 'Isa Khan, and my family was in Rohtas, while I accompanied Sher Khan to the hills." When Sher Khan got possession of Rohtas, he left there his women and children, with his eldest son Adil Khan, and Kutb Khan; and he himself went to the hills of Bahrkunda, and wandered about from place to place.[39]

After the Emperor Humayun had got possession of Chunar he halted in Benares, and sent an envoy to Sher

which they seldom bestowed upon their patrons for deeds of a much more heinous nature.—See Dorn, p. 109.

[39] Ahmad Yadgar (MS. pp. 170-5) mentions an expedition against the Raja of Jharkand, in order to secure possession of a favourite white elephant, called "Syam Chandar," which had the "peculiarity of never throwing dust upon its head." This was duly obtained, along with other plunder, and brought to Sher Shah, who chose to consider it as an omen that he should one day obtain the Empire of Dehli. [It is odd that a *white* elephant should have been called *syam,* i.e. *black.*]

Khan, having it in view to get possession of the country of Bihar. Sher Khan knew he had this design, and said to the envoy, "I have captured the fort of Gaur, and have collected about me a very large force of Afghans. If the Emperor will abandon all design upon Bengal, I will surrender Bihar to him, and make it over to whomsoever he will depute, and will agree to the same boundaries of Bengal as existed in Sultan Sikandar's time; and I will send all the ensigns of royalty—as the umbrella throne, etc.—to the Emperor, and will yearly send his ten *lacs* of rupees from Bengal. But let the Emperor return towards Agra." The envoy came back to Humayun, and reported what Sher Khan said. The Emperor, on hearing about Bihar, became exceedingly glad, and agreed to what Sher Khan proposed, and gave a horse, and a peculiarly splendid *khil'at* to the envoy for delivery to Sher Shah; and directed him to say to Sher Shah that his proposals were accepted, and that he should not delay to put them in execution. The *vakil* came to Sher Shah, and gave him the horse and dress, and told him what the Emperor had said. Sher Khan was much delighted, and said, "I will fulfill the terms agreed upon and will pray day and night to Almighty God that while life lasts no hostility may befall between the Emperor and myself, for I am his dependent and servant."

Three days after this despatch the envoy of Sultan Mahmud, the ruler of Bengal, came into the presence of the Emperor Humayun, and made the following communication: "The Afghans have seized the fort of Gaur, but most of the country is yet in my possession; let not Your Majesty trust to Sher Khan's promises, but march towards these parts, and before they have established and strengthened themselves, expel them from the country, and altogether suppress this revolt. I also will join you, and they are not powerful enough to oppose you." As soon as he heard this request of Sultan Mahmud, the Emperor ordered his victorious standards to be set in motion towards Bengal; and afterwards he ordered the Khan-khanan Yusuf-khail, the Birlas chiefs and some other nobles, to go on in advance, and with their force in battle array to move towards the hills of Bahrkunda, where Sher Khan was. Mirza Hindal also was ordered to cross the Ganges with his division and to move on Hajipur. The Emperor himself went towards Bengal.

When Sher Khan heard this intelligence, he entirely gave up all trust in the promises and faith of Humayun, and said to the envoy: "I have observed all loyalty to the Emperor, and have committed no offence against him, and have not encroached upon his boundaries. When I got Bihar from the Lohanis, and the King of Bengal formed a design to seize that country, I besought him most submissively to leave me as I was, and not to attempt to deprive me of Bihar. By reason of his large army and forces he would not attend to me, and since he thus oppressed me, the Almighty gave me the victory; and as he coveted the kingdom of Bihar, God wrested away from him also the kingdom of Bengal. The Emperor has only considered the word of the ruler of Bengal, and has overlooked the service I have rendered, and all the force of Afghans which I have assembled for his service, and has marched against Bengal. When the Emperor besieged Chunar, the Afghans urged me to oppose him, but I restrained them from declaring war and said, 'The Emperor is powerful; you should not fight with him for the sake of a fort, for he is my lord and patron, and when he perceives that, in spite of my powerful forces, I pay respect to him, he will understand that I am his loyal servant, and will give me a kingdom to maintain this large army. The Emperor desired the kingdom of Bihar, and I was willing to surrender it. But it is not the right way to govern a kingdom to separate so large a force from his service, and in order to please their enemies, to ruin and slay the Afghans.' But since the Emperor takes no heed of all this good service, and has violated his promise, I have now no hope or means of restraining the Afghans from opposing him. You will hear what deeds the Afghans will do, and the march to Bengal will end in repentance and regret, for now the Afghans are united, and have laid aside their mutual quarrels and envyings. The country which the Mughals have taken from the Afghans, they got through the internal dissensions among the latter." So saying, he gave him a parting present, and dismissed him. The force he had with him Sher Khan sent to Rohtas, and he himself with a few horsemen, in order that he might not be traced, set off from that place towards Gaur secretly. From thence he proceeded, unknown to any one, to the hills, and lay hid there and sent spies into the camp of the Emperor in order to discover his intentions. Humayun was told, after he had made two marches that Sher Khah had gone to the hills. He therefore, returned and the Khan-khanan Yusuf-khail and Barri Birlas, who had been sent against Sher Khan, were halted in the *pargana* of Munir Shaik Yahya, where they heard that Sultan Mahmud Barri, the King of Gaur, was come. Birlas went out to meet him. They had not yet escorted him to his encamping ground, when the Emperor himself arrived at Munir. They brought Sultan Mahmud to the Emperor, who did not receive him kindly or pay him the respect he anticipated; so that Sultan Mahmud repented that he had come and shortly afterwards died from extreme grief. The Emperor issued orders for the arrangement of his army at the town of Munir.

Muyid Beg, son of Sultan Mahmud, and Jahangir Kuli, son of Ibrahim Bayazid, Mir Nurka, Tardi Beg, Barri Birlas, Mubarak Farmuli, and other chiefs, with a force of 30,000 horse, were ordered to march seven *kos* in advance of the Imperial army. Sher Khan, on hearing that Humayun had set off towards Bengal departed himself secretly with only a few horsemen. When the Emperor reached Patna, the division which was seven *kos* in advance had not reached their ground, when their vedettes came to a village where what should they see but some cavalry in a garden. They asked of one of the villagers whose those horsemen were? He said, "It is Sher Khan himself." The vedettes, when they heard the name of Sher Khan, were so alarmed, that they never examined what amount of force Sher Khan had with him, but returned and told to Muyid Beg that "Sher Khan was encamped at such and such a village. Muyid Beg was of opinion that Sher Khan was there to oppose them, and sent to the Emperor to ask for orders; and encamped where he was, sending out a reconnoitring party to bring intelligence. When the persons sent to reconnoitre came near the place, they could not discover a single horseman there; on which the Mughals entered the village, and inquired of the head man (*mukaddam*), who said, that Sher Khan had halted there with a few horsemen; but on seeing the advance of their cavalry had gone off with all speed on the road to Mungir. When the party returned from reconnoitring, it was nearly evening, and on this account they delayed the pursuit of Sher Khan.

When Sher Khan had crossed the defile of Ghari, he saw Saif Khan Acha-khail Sarwani, who was taking his family towards Rohtas. Sher Khan said, "Turn, for the Mughal army is near at hand." When Saif Khan was apprised of the actual truth regarding the Emperor's army, he said to Sher Khan, "There are but few men with you, and the distance between the armies is small. The Emperor will pursue you with the utmost expedition, in the hope you may fall into his hands. Do you take my family with you, and go your way. Early to-morrow morning I will occupy the entrance of the pass, and while life remains in my body I will hold the Emperor's army in check, so that an ample distance may be placed between you and the Mughals." Sher Khan said, "It is not right that to preserve myself I should cast you into the whirlpool of destruction." Saif Khan replied: "All men are not equal; a man ought to sacrifice himself for his own household....... My life and those of my brethren shall be expended in the service of my lord." Although Sher Khan urged him repeatedly to go along with him, Saif Khan would not consent; so Sher Khan took his family with him, and relieved from all anxiety regarding the pursuit of the Mughals, proceded on his course with all speed.

The next morning, when the sun was well risen, Saif Khan told his brethren to bathe, and he prepared for death. . . . Saif Khan's brethren said: "Since you have decided to do this, we are ready to sacrifice a thousand lives for you; it is the time now to act, not to talk; we will not fail to do our best. On this they put themselves at their several posts, and occupied the entrance of Gugarghar. When the army of the Emperor drew near, Saif Khan commenced the action. Notwithstanding great exertions on the part of the Mughals, they could not force the entrance of Gugarghar. The gallantry displayed by Saif Khan's brethren was beyond all description; they held the Mughals in check till a little after mid-day, when most of Saif Khan's brethren were slain, and he himself was severely wounded in three places; and becoming insensible, was taken alive by the Mughals. They took him before Myyid, who sent him to the Emperor; and he, when he heard his story, praised him very highly, saying, "Such it behoves a soldier to be, who should lay down his life to advance his master's interests." He then said to Saif Khan. "I set you free, go whither you please." Saif Khan said, "My family is with Sher Khan, I wish to go to him." The Emperor replied: "I have given you your life, do as you will. So Saif Khan returned to Sher Khan.

When Sher Khan arrived at Mungir, where Shuja'at

Khan Niazi[40] was, he ordered him as Humayun's army was approaching, to take Saif Khan's family to the fort of Ghari, and embarking in a swift sailing boat, went down the river towards Gaur. When he arrived there, he sent his son Jalal Khan with some of his nobles to occupy the pass of Ghari,[41] and to hold the Emperor Humayun in check there, while he himself made all necessary preparations and arrangements, and conveyed to Rohtas the treasure which had fallen into his possession at Gaur. When Jalal Khan came to Ghari, the van of the Emperor's army was already near at hand. Jalal Khan proposed to attack it but his chief dissuaded him, saying that he had not been sent by Sher Khan to risk an engagement, and that he ought merely to hold the pass against Humayun's advance. Jalal Khan, however, did not assent to their counsel, but leaving 1000 horse to hold Ghari, and advancing himself with 6000 attacked the Imperialists, and after a sharp action defeated them.[42] Mubarak Farmuli, Abu-l Fath Langah, as well as many men on the side of the Mughals, fell in the engagement.[43]

Jalal Khan, returning to Ghari, fortified the pass. The night after the action it rained so hard, that the

[40] "Thana" in one MS.

[41] "Which" adds Nia'matu-lla, who calls it Garhi, "is the only passage to the countries of Gaur and Bengal; there being except by that gate, no other way of entry or exit"—*Makhzan-i Afghani*, MS. p. 202. It is now better known as "Sicly-gully", properly Sankri-gali, the narrow pass about eight miles, north-west from Rajmahal. It is incorrect to call it the only passage into Bengal, for the Mahrattas, in 1742, penetrated through another to the south-west, to say nothing of others.

[42] One MS. has: "But although there was much fighting, did not defeat the Emperor's force."

[43] Some further details will be found among the extracts from the *Makhzan-i-Afghani*.

road was rendered impassable, for it was the commencement of the rainy season. The Emperor was delayed in this spot one month, and Sher Khan availing himself of the interval, and taking with him all the treasure which had come into his hands by the fall of Gaur, went by way of Jharkand to Rohtas; and on arrving there, sent to Jalal Khan, directing him to abandon Ghari and to come to Rohtas. When the Emperor heard that Jalal Khan had abandoned and gone away from Ghari, he sent (on account of the excessive rain) a part of his force under Mirza Hindal to Agra, and proceeded himself to Gaur, the capital of Bengal, where he lay[1] for three months, and admitted no one to an audience with him. A. H. 945 (A.D. 1538-9).

Meanwhile, Sher Khan came to Benares, and besieged the governor, and detached thence Khawas Khan to Mungir, where the Emperor had left the Khan-khanan Yusuf Khail, when he himself went to Gaur. Sher Khan sent Khawas Khan with instructions to take Khan-khanan prisoner, and bring him to his presence, because this same Khan-khanan had brought the Emperor Babar from Kabul to India. Khawas Khan came suddenly by night upon the city and seizing the Khan-khanan, brought him to Benares. Shortly after this, Benares was taken, and the greater part of the Mughal garrison was killed. Subsequently, Haibat Khan Niazi, Jalal Khan Jalu, Sarmast Khan Sarwani, and other chiefs were sent against Bahraich, and they drove out the Mughals from those parts until they arrived at and captured the city of Sambhal, and made slaves of the inhabitants, and spoiled the city. Another force was sent towards Jaunpur, the governor of which place was killed in battle, and the same force was then sent in the direction of Agra. Every governor on the part of the Emperor Humayun, throughout the whole country, who offered any opposition, was killed, or was defeated and driven out of the country; so that all the districts as far as Kanauj and

Sambhal fell into the possession of the Afghans. Sher Khan also sent Khawas Khan against the city of Maharta, *zamindar,* with orders to cut down his jungle fastness, and to capture him. The officers of Sher Khan also collected the revenue of both the autumn and spring harvests of these parts.

When the Emperor heard that Mirza Hindal had slain Shaikh Bahlol, and excited a sedition in the neighbourhood of Agra, he became distracted,[44] and started from Bengal (as the heat of the season had somewhat abated) towards Agra. Sher Khan, summoning all his forces from Bihar, Jaunpur, and other places, excepting only the division with Khawas Khan acting against Maharta,[45] collected them in the environs of the fort of Rohtas.

When the Emperor Humayun advanced in the direction of Sher Khan, thus encamped about Rohtas, Sher Khan assembled his chiefs and addressed them thus: "The army of the Emperor Humayun is in great disorder from his delay in Bengal; moreover, sedition has arisen in Agra. It is on this account that he neglects me and is taking his departure. If you agree with me, I will try my fortune, for my force at this moment is

[44] Because, as stated in the *Makhzan-i Afghani,* the Shaikh was a man unequalled in erudition and piety, and the Emperor was personally much attached to him. The Shaikh had been sent by Humayun to Hindal, to admonish him against his ambitious designs.—See Dorn, p. 116.

[45] "Who, whenever Sher Khan was in any trouble, used to descend from his hills and jungles and harass the tenants around Bihar; and taking to highway robbery, closed the road to travellers proceeding to Gaur and Bengal, and took every opportunity of plundering horses, camels and bullocks from the camp of Sher Khan. Therefore, his extermination being considered urgently necessary, Khawas Khan was not summoned." *Makhzan-i Afghani* MS., p. 208. Dorn, p. 116.

in perfect order. Before the Emperor marched against Bengal I made every submission, and agreed to pay a yearly tribute, if the Emperor would confer Bengal on me, that I might not be brought into hostilities with my patron. He agreed to give me Bengal, but when the envoy of the King of Bengal, Sultan Maḥmud, came to him, the king retracted his promise, and I was compelled to oppose him; and now that I have overthrown his armies which were in Bihar and Jaunpur, and taken those countries, the way to peace is closed." 'Azam Humayun Sarwani (who had been one of Sikandar's nobles, and had now joined himself to Sher Khan) replied: "You ought not to take counsel with the nobles of Sultans Bahlol and Sikandar as to fighting the Mughals for this reason, that every plan we have devised has by our ill-fortune failed, and as often as we have fought, we have from our internal dissensions been defeated. Fortune has befriended you, in that the whole of the Afghans have become united heart and soul under you, and have been always ready to engage the Mughals. Men of experience and sagacity have declared to me that the Afghans are not inferior to the Mughals in warlike prowess, but fly away only because of their internal disunion. The Afghans will drive the Mughals from India, whenever they obey one leader and are united under him. You are that fortunate man. Ask your other chiefs and act on their advice; as for us, victory has become your friend, and I have nothing to recommend."

When Sher Khan heard these words of 'Azam Humayun, he asked his other nobles, for example, Kutb Khan, Haibat Khan Niazi, Jalal Khan bin Jaloi, Shuja'at Khan, Sarmast Khan Sarwani, and others; and they unanimously declared that it was advisable to fight, for they would never have such an opportunity again.

When Sher Khan perceived that the Afghans were united in his favour and in good heart to fight the Mughals, he quitted the hills of Rohtas, and marched to meet the Emperor's army. At every stage he entrenched himself with an earthwork, and going on entirely at his leisure, made very short marches. When the Emperor heard that Sher Khan was coming, he retracted his steps, and turned in the direction of Sher Khan's army. Sher Khan on hearing this, wrote to the Emperor, saying, that if the Emperor would give him the kingdom of Bengal, and be satisfied that the *khutba* be read and money struck in the Emperor's name, he would be the Emperor's vassal. Sher Khan then marching on, and selecting an advantageous place,—a large village with a stream of water intervening between himself and the Empeor,—entrenched himself there.[46] The breadth of the stream was twenty-five yards.

Khawas Khan also, who had been sent against Maharta, was summoned to come with all speed. The Emperor, on receiving Sher Khan's missive, agreed to give him the kingdom of Bengal, but on condition that whereas he had transgressed his boundaries, and had encamped himself in face of the Emperor on the other side the stream, he should show his respect to the Emperor by retreating, and leaving the passage of the river free to the Emperor; and that when the Emperor Humayun had crossed, he would march two or three marches in the track of Sher Khan, and then turn back.[47] Sher

[46] Nia'matu-lla indicates the place with greater exactness: "Sher Khan pitched his own opposite the royal camp, at a village called Shataya, between Jhusa (Chaunsa) and Baksar, so that both armies were encamped on the same side of the Ganges. There was also a small stream flowing between the two camps, of which the banks were so steep, that it could not be crossed except at the usual ford." *Makhzan-i-Afghani*, MS., p. 212 (Dorn, p. 118).

[47] This silly manœuvre is also mentioned by Nia'matu-lla; it was to be a feigned pursuit, in order to save appearances.—Dorn. p. 120.

Khan agreed to these conditions, and leaving the passage of the river free, retraced his march. The Emperor bridging the river, crossed it with his whole camp and army and family, and pitched on the further side.

He then sent Shaikh Khalil, a descendant[48] of Shaik Farid Shakar-ganj (the pole of the world), on an embassy to Sher Khan, to urge him to march by regular states back to Rohtas, and to delay nowhere, and to promise that the Emperor, after making some marches in his rear, would turn aside, and after that would give, as he had agreed, to Sher Khan's agent, a *farman* for the kingdom of Bengal. When Shaikh Khalil came to Sher Khan, he told him what the Emperor had said. Sher Khan ostensibly agreed to this arrangement, and received him with all honour and hospitality; nor did he omit the slightest point of customary etiquette. Shaikh Khalil, in the presence of the Emperor's men who had accompanied him, debated earnestly and long with Sher Shah, and strongly advised the proposed peace; and during the consultation the following words fell from Shaikh Khalil: "If you do not agree to peace, away with you; declare war, and fight." Sher Khan said "What you say is a good omen for me; please God, I will fight." After the consultation. Sher Khan gave to Shaikh Khalil money and rich clothes and manufactures of Malda and of Bengal in enormous quantities, and captivated his heart by these presents and favours. Sher Khan then sent for Shaikh Khalil in private, and speaking of the reverence the Afghans entertained for the holy Shaikh

[48] The original has *farzand,* literally "a son". The *Tarkikh-i Khan Jahan* (MS. p. 190) has *nabira,* "grandson." The latter work entirely exonerates Shaik Khalil from the charge of the perfidy, by representing him as the agent, not of Humayun, but of Sher Shah, who was his spiritual pupil. So does Ahmed Yadar (MS. p. 279), and Firishta (Briggs. vol. ii., p. 37). This is by far more probable than the statement in the text.

Farid Shakar-ganj, and of their mutual fatherland, and making him promises to his heart's content, said, "I wish you to give me advice regarding peace or war with the Emperor Humayun for the learned have said, 'It behoves one to take counsel with the wise, with the intelligent, and with far-seeing holy men.' Now, in you all these qualifications are united. Tell me, therefore, without diminution or reserve, what your mind, clear as the sun, thinks concerning my well-being. Is peace or war with the Emperor most to my advantage?" After much hesitation, Shaikh Khalil said, "By asking my advice, you have in two ways placed me in a great difficulty; first, since I have come to you as an envoy from the Emperor, it is not right that I should say anything except to his advantage; and, secondly, you have asked advice from me, and those of old have said, 'If even your enemy asks your advice, speak the truth.' If I give advice contrary to my own opinion, I shall act dishonestly. The Afghans for generations past have held my ancestors in reverence; and it appears from the miraculous precepts of the holy prophet Muhammad (may God's mercy rest on him!), that it behoves him who gives advice to do so in good faith. I am compelled, therefore, to speak the truth. War with the Emperor Humayun is more for your advantages than peace; for this reason, that in his army the most complete disorder exists, he has no horses or cattle, and his own brothers are in rebellion against him. He only makes peace with you now from necessity, and will not eventually abide by the treaty. Look on this opportunity as so much gained, and do not let it out of your grasp, for you will never again have such another." Sher Khan was wavering in his decision as to peace or war; but as Shaikh Khalil advised against the peace, he abandoned all idea of it, and determined on war. He had before sent for Khawas Khan, and when he arrived he ordered the whole of this troops to arms, as if Maharta was approaching to attack them.

When he had gone four *kos* out of his encampment he returned, saying the spies had reported that Maharta was yet distant.

The next day he again arrayed his army and moved out, and when he had gone several *kos*, returned, and said that Maharta was not coming that day. A little before midnight he assembled all his chiefs, and said, "I have promised peace to the Emperor Humayun; but I have considered that all the good service I have rendered has produced no good fruit; and after all my loyalty to him in producing the defeat of Sultan Mahmud. he demanded from me the fort of Chunar. When I refused to yield it, he sent a force to take it; and when that failed, he came himself to seize the fort by force, but abandoned his intentions when he heard that Mirza Muhammad Zaman had escaped from prison and had raised a sedition in the country. Moreover, Sultan Bahadur, King of Gujarat, was coming to invade the country of Dehli, and so he was compelled to return. I sent my son Kutb Khan with him throughout the Gujarat campaign.[49] Though I could have taken possession of the country of Jaunpur, etc. yet I did not commit any act of hostility, for the Emperor is mighty; and though I had the power, I would not do any disloyal and evil act, that the Emperor might perceive I was his faithful servant and desist from seeking to injure me. When he returned from Gujarat, he got his army in readiness, and without regarding my loyalty, did his best to expel me; but as my fortune was great, he did not achieve his desire. I made every submission, but it was all profitless. When, in violation of his promises, he attacked Bengal, I lost all hope in his goodness, and apprehending evil from him, was compelled to declare hostilities

[49] "Accompanied by 5000 valiant horsemen skilled in the use of the sabre."—*Makhzan-i Afghani*, MS., p. 216. Others give the more probable amount of 500.

against him, and I expelled his governors and spoiled his country as far as Sambhal, and have not left a single Mughal in those parts. Now, with what hope can I conclude this peace with him? He makes peace and manifests a friendly disposition towards me, because his army is in want of horses and cattle and of every equipment, and because his brothers have rebelled against him. He is but playing with me, and eventually will not abide by this peace; but having appeased the rebellion of his brothers on his arrival at Agra, and refurnished his army, he will not fail to uproot and destroy me. I have often experienced that the Afghans are braver in battle than the Mughals, who only got the country from the dissensions of the Afghans. If my brothers advise so, I will break off the peace, and will try my fortune." They all replied: "By your blessing, dissension has been banished from among the Afghan nation, and we all have been cherished by you; we will not fail in devotion and gallantry to our utmost capability. Your purpose of breaking off the treaty is most wise." Sher Khan said, 'I break off the treaty. I have put my trust in the Protector, and will fight the Emperor Humayun, as Mian Nizami has observed." . . . . When he dismissed the chiefs, he ordered them to array their men with all speed as if they were still in alarm as to Maharta; and when one watch of the night yet remained, the whole army, according to Sher Khan's command, marched two and a half *kos* in the direction of Maharta's country. Sher Khan then halted, and addressed his army, saying, "For two days I have drawn out my army, and have returned to my encampment, that I might put the Emperor off his guard, and that he might not suspect that my army was coming towards him. Now, turn; set your faces towards the army of the Emperor, and let not the honour of the Afghans out of your grasp nor fail to display your utmost devotion, for now is the time to regain the Empire of Hindustan." The Afghans replied "Let not our lord allow any hesitation to find its way to his noble heart." . . . .

Having read the *fatiha,* and drawn up his forces in order of battle, Sher Shah with all haste marched towards the Emperor's camp. When the Afghans were close at hand, news was brought to the Emperor that Sher Khan was coming with all speed to battle with him. The Emperor ordered out his army to resist the attack, saying that after a short delay, and having performed his ablutions, he also would follow. The Emperor was a lion (in valour), and in the excess of his gallantry and daring. . . . . So from the pride of youth, and confidence in the multitude of his forces and followers, who had no equals for intrepidity and gallantry, he despised the forces of Sher Shah, who were all Afghans, and did not even inspect his forces nor pay regard to what is necessary in an engagement; nor did he take into consideration the disorganization which the climate of Bengal had produced in his army. Sher Khan knew all the devices and stratagems of war, and knew how to commence and conclude an engagement, and had experienced both prosperity and misfortune. The army of the Mughals had not extricated themselves from their camp, before the Afghan army were already upon them, and coming boldly on, atacked the army of the Emperor without hesitation. In the twinkling of an eye they routed the Mughal forces. Humayun had not completed his ablutions when the intelligence reached him that the Mughals were utterly scattered, so that to rally them was impossible. The confusion in the army was so great that he had no time to remove his family, but fled in the direction of Agra, with the intention of collecting all his forces at that place, and returning again from thence to destroy his enemy.

Masnad Ali Haibat Khan told me 'Abbas Khan, the author of this book, that he was at Sher Khan's side when the Emperor Humayun's queen, with other noble ladies and a crowd of women, came out from behind the *parda*. As soon as Sher Khan's eye fell upon them, he alighted off his horse, and showed them every respect and consoled them.[50] He then performed a special ablution, and returned twofold thanks to the Lord of Eternity, and raising up his hands in prayer with all humility and with tears, said. . . . After this he sent the heralds to proclaim throughout the army that no person should make captives of or keep a Mughal woman, child, or female slave in his tent one night, but should bring them all to the queen's encampment, and the strictness of his command carried such authority among the Afghans that no person had any power to resist it; and the heralds before night brought all the wives and families of the Mughals to the queen's encampment and assigned rations to each person. Sher Khan some days afterwards sent the queen to Rohtas under charge of Hussain Khan Nirak, and providing the families of the other Mughals with carriages and their necessary expenses, sent them on towards Agra.[51]

Sher Khan, who had assumed the title of "Hazrat Ali" since the star of victory had risen in the horizon of his good fortune, ordered his *munshis* to write letters descriptive of his victory to all parts of the country which were in his possession. Masnad Ali Isa Khan, son of Umar Khan, whose title was "Khan-i'azam," and who during the time Sultan Bahlol after the death of Tatar Khan Yusuf-khail, held Lahore in *jagir*, said to Sher Khan, "You should write the letters describing your victory in the style of *farmans*." Sher Khan observed: "You, who formerly were nobles of Sultans Bahlol and

[50] Some further particulars respecting this defeat will be found among the Extracts from the *Makhzan-i Afghani*, and under the reign of Humayun. The date assigned by Niamatu-lla is Muharram. 946.

[51] Ahmad Yadgar (MS. p. 284) says there were no less than 4,000 Mughal women.

Sikandar, have for the cause of the Afghans, done me the honour of joining yourselves to me. It does not become me to send *farmans* to you, and to seat myself on the throne while you stand around me. The king of Hindustan has escaped alive, and still holds most of the country in his possession." Isa Khan explained that he had a great desire to seat Sher Khan upon the throne, and said, "Sultan Sikandar and his descendants who, out of regard to their clansmen, would not ascend the throne, acted in violation of the custom of kings. It behoves him whom God Almighty brings to empire, and elevates and exalts above the rest of mankind, to observe the rules of etiquette of former princes." . . . . After this, 'Azam Humayun Sarwani, said "The Mughals have been kings for two descents; they despise the Afghans. and consider them as not their own equals in the day of battle; yet by the excellence of your wisdom and your conquering fortune, the Afghans have overthrown them." . . . . Mian Babin Lodi and the other Afghans with one consent cried: "There are none like Masnad Ali Kalkapur[52] Sarwani and 'Azam Humayun Sarwani in the army of the Afghans; what they have said is most right; it is not good to delay." Sher Khan was much delighted, and said "The kingly name is a very exalted thing, and is not devoid of trouble; but since the noble minds of my friends have decided to make me king, I agree." He ordered the astrologers to fix an auspicious moment for his ascent to the throne. When they had consulted the calendar, they came with great delight and said, "An auspicious moment, by the good fortune of your birth hour, has now come. If you at this moment seat yourself upon the throne, defeat and rout will never show their face in your victorious army." He seated himself on the throne, unfolded the umbrella over his head, and assumed the name of Sher

[52] (Var. "Kaknur." "Kalnur," "Laknur".)

Shah, and struck coin and caused the *khutba* to be read in his own name; and he took also the additional title of "Shah Alam."[53] He said to 'Isa Khan, "You are the son of Shaikh Malani, and have induced me to strike coin and have the *khutba* read in my own name; write one letter descriptive of the victory, with your own hand, the *munshis* will write the rest." So 'Isa Khan wrote one copy with his own hand, and the *munshis* wrote the rest. For seven days drums were beaten in token of rejoicing; and the young men of the Afghan army came in crowds from every tribe and danced, as is the custom of the Afghans. . . . . .

Sher Khan himself pursued the Emperor Humayun, and got possession of the whole country as far as Kalpi and Kanauj. He again sent Khawas Khan against Maharta Cheruh,[54] to utterly destroy him. Jahangir Kuli Beg, with 6,000 cavalry, was in Bengal; him he ordered to be put to death,[55] and the chiefs of Hind who were with the Emperor Humayun he let go free; but Shaikh Khalil he kept, and made him one of his own friends and counsellors. He sent 'Isa Khan towards Gujarat and Mandu, and to the chiefs of those parts he wrote, saying, "I am about to send a son of mine into your neighbourhood. When the Emperor Humayun moves towards Kanauj, do you accompany my son, and seize and lay waste the country about Agra and Dehli. At that time a certain man, by name Mallu Khan, had

[53] (The Waki'at-i-Mushtaki gives the same title, but from his coins it would appear that it was "Sultanu-l' 'Adil." See Thomas's *Chronicles of the Pathan Kings*, p. 395).

[54] (Var. "Jaru.")

[55] The *Makhzan-i-Afghani* adds, that Jalal Khan Jaloi and Haji Khan Batni were sent to Bengal; and after defeating Jahangir Kuli, the governor, who was at the head of 6,000 horse, Bengal fell again under the dominion of the Afghans.

made himself king in Mandu, Sarangpur, and Ujjain, and had assumed the name of Kadir Shah; and in Raisin and Chanderi, Bhaia Puran Mall ruled as deputy of the infant Raja Partab, son of Bhupat Shah, the son of Salahu-d din. In Sewas, Sikandar Khan Miana held sway; and Mahesar was Raja of Bhopal. These rulers of Malwa wrote in reply, that when Sher Shah's son came to those parts, they would not fail to assist and serve him. Mallu Khan put his seal at the head of the letter which he sent, and when the letter arrived, Sher Shah tore up the letter and put the seal in his turban (by way of showing respect ironically).

When 'Isa Khan went to Gujarat, Sultan Mahmud was a minor; but his minister Darya Khan wrote that the king was a minor, the chiefs at enmity among themselves, and that the Khan-khanan Yusuf-khail had taken away with him all the army of Mandu and Gujarat. 'Isa Khan observed to Sher Shah that "wherever misfortunes have befallen the Afghans from the Mughals, it has been through this man. The Khan-khanan Yusuf-khail brought the Emperor Babar into India from Kabul; and if the Emperor Humayun had acted according to what the Khan-khanan advised, he would not have repented it, and would have utterly destroyed you; but your good fortune prevailed, so that the Emperor did not act upon his advice. He must be put to death, for it is not right to allow him to live, even though he be a prisoner (at Mungir)." Sher Shah said, "Every Afghan whom I have consulted has said, 'He is an Afghan of consideration, and it is not advisable to kill him'. But my opinion has been that which 'Isa Khan has expressed." So he gave orders that the Khan-khanan, who had been kept in confinement since his capture at Mungir, and who had received a daily allowance of half a *sir* of unground barley, should be put to death; so he was slain. News arrived that Emperor Humayun purposed marching towards Kanauj. Sher

Khan despatched his son, by name Kutb Khan, to Mandu, in order that he might, in concert with the chiefs of those parts, alarm and ravage the country about Agra and Dehli. When the Emperor Humayun heard that Sher Shah had sent his son towards Chanderi, that he might raise disturbances in those parts, he sent both his brothers, Mirza Hindal and Mirza 'Askari, with other nobles, in that direction. When the Malwa chiefs heard that two brothers of the Emperor were coming to oppose Kutb Khan, they gave him no assistance. Kutb Khan went from Chanderi to the city of Chondha, and engaging the Mughals at Chondha,[56] was slain. Mirza Hindal and Mirza Askari having gained this victory, returned to the Emperor.

When Sher Shah heard that the chiefs of the country of Mandu had not assisted Kutb Khan, and that Kutb Khan was slain, he was extremely grieved and enraged; nevertheless, he did not openly manifest this by his conduct, but kept his grudge against the chiefs of Mandu concealed in his own bosom. The Mughals gained excessive confidence from this victory, and large forces having come also from their own country, the Emperor Humayun arrayed his army and came to Kanauj (Zi-l ka'da, 946 A.H. April, 1540 A.D.) Sher Shah also fortified himself on the opposite side of the river Ganges. At this conjuncture he received intelligence that Khawas Khan had slain Maharta. There was great rejoicing in the Afghan army[57], and Sher Shah wrote to Khawas,

[56] (This name is a very doubtful one.) The Timurian authors put this engagement at Kalpi.

[57] Great importance appears always to have been attached to this conquest. In the *Waki'at-i Mushtaki*. (MS. p. 110) we find it mentioned, towards the close of Sher Shah's reign, that the three great works accomplished by him were, the destruction of the infidel Maharta, the massacre of the idolaters of Raisin, and the re-establishment of Islam in Nagor, by the expulsion of Maldeo.

saying: "Come with all speed to me; for I and your other friends are awaiting your coming before we engage the enemy; we are looking anxiously in your direction." And when he heard of the near approach of Khawas Khan, he sent a herald to the Emperor Humayun, saying, "I have for some time entrenched myself here. The Emperor has the power to choose. If he will cross the river he may fight with me on this side; or, if he prefer it, I will cross the river, and fight with the Emperor on that side." When the herald came to the Emperor, and reported what Sher Shah had said, the Emperor, in utter contempt of Sher Shah, replied: "Say to Sher Khan that if he will retreat some *kos* from the waterside, I will cross the river Ganges and give him battle." The herald returned and told Sher Shah what the Emperor had said. Sher Shah retreated several *kos* from the river bank. The Emperor Humayun having prepared a bridge, crossed the river Ganges. Hamid Khan Kakar, one of Sher Shah's nobles, said, "You ought to attack the Mughal army before they have all crossed the river." Sher Shah replied: "I have never before had any advantages, and have been compelled to use stratagems in warfare. Now by the favour of the all-powerful, my force is not inferior to the Emperor's. I will not now, notwithstanding my advantages, break my promise in the face of day. With my army arrayed in the open field, I will give battle without fraud or stratagem. God's will, whatever it may be, will be manifested." When Sher Shah understood that the whole force of the Emperor was across the river, he returned towards it, and carefully throwing up, according to his custom, an earthwork embankment opposite the Emperor's army, encamped close by it.

"If God please! these three deeds will secure his salvation." The supineness of Sultan Ibrahim had occasioned the two latter to triumph for a time, but Sher Shah had never ceased to pray for their extermination.

After some days Khawas Khan also came; on the very day he arrived, Sher Shah marched in fighting order, and captured all the supplies which were coming to the Emperor's army, and took 300 camels, and a large convoy of bullocks. On the 10th Muharram, 947 H., both armies drew out their forces. Sher Shah thus arranged his army. In the centre was Sher Shah himself, with Haibat Khan Niazi, who bore the title of 'Azam Humayun, Masnad 'Ali 'Isa Khan Sarwani, Kutb Khan Lodi, Haji Khan Jaloi, Buland Khan, Sarmast Khan, Saif Khan Sarwani, Bijli Khan, and others. On the right were Jalal Khan, son of Sher Shah, who after Sher Shah's death succeeded him on the throne, and was entitled Islam Shah, Taj Khan, Sulaiman Khan Kirani, Jalal Khan Jaloi and others. On the left, 'Adil Khan, son of Sher Shah, Kutb Khan, Rai Husain Jalwani, and others. When Sher Shah had drawn up his army in this order, he said to the Afghans: "I have used my best exertions to collect you together, I have done my best in training you, and have kept you in anticipation of such a day as this. This is the day of trial; whoever of you shows himself to excel in valour on the field of battle, him will I promote above his fellows." . . . . The Afghans replied: "The mighty king has much protected and favoured us. This is the time for us to serve him and show our devotion." Sher Shah ordered each chief to return to his own followers, and to remain with them; and he himself went through the army and set it in proper array.

The Emperor's forces were broken by Khawas Khan's division, but Sher Shah's right, under his son Jalal Khan, was defeated: four of the chiefs, however, kept their ground, such as Jalal Khan himself, Mian Aiyub Kalkapur Sarwani, and Ghazi Mujli. When Sher Shah saw that his right was broken, he wished to go to its assistance; but Kutb Khan Lodi said: "My lord, do not quit your own post, lest men should think the centre also is broken. Go on into the midst of the enemy." As Sher Shah's division proceeded straight on, they encountered the Mughal force which had routed Sher Shah's right; they defeated and drove it on the Emperor's centre division. Sher Shah having driven away the Mughal force in front of his son Jalal Khan; and his left, in which was his other son Adil Khan and Kutb Khan Banet, having repulsed the troops opposed to them, fell on the Mughal centre. Sher Shah's right, which had been defeated, rallied at the same time, and thus the Afghan army completely surrounded the Mughal force. Sher Shah's sons and other Afghan chiefs performed many gallant acts, especially Haibat Khan Niazi, and Khawas Khan, who drove back the Mughals with the stroke of the watered sabre and the point of the life-melting spear. The Emperor Humayun himself remained firm like a mountain in his position on the battle-field, and displayed such valour and gallantry as is beyond all description. . . .

When the Emperor saw supernatural beings fighting against him, he acknowledged the work of God, abandoned the battle to these unearthly warriors, and turned the bridle of his purpose towards his capital of Agra. He received no wound himself, and escaped safe and sound out of that bloodthirsty whirlpool. The greater part of his army was driven into the river Ganges.[58]. . . Sher Shah being at his ease regarding the Mughals, wrote to Shuja'at Khan, whom he had left as *faujdar,* in the country of Bihar and Rohtas, to besiege the fort of

[58] The *Makhzan-i Afghani* (MS., p. 229) and *Tarikh-i Khan Jahan* (MS., p. 161), represent that there was a bridge, which was broken by the excessive pressure upon it during the retreat. All authorities concur in saying there was a bridge by which the Imperialists crossed to the eastern side, but few mention it on the retreat. The Emperor himself fled on an elephant which swam the river with difficulty.

Gwalior, and he told the bearer of the *farman*: "The son of Shuja'at Khan, by name Mahmud Khan, has been slain; do not tell him before he has quitted Rohtas, lest on hearing of the death of his son he delays and puts off his coming." As soon as he received the *farman*, Shuja'at Khan went and besieged Gwalior.[59] From Kanauj Sher Shah despatched Barmazid Gur with a large force in advance, but directed him not to hazard an engagement with the Emperor Humayun, and he also sent another force under Nasir Khan towards Sambhal. Having speedily settled the country about Kanauj, he betook himself in the direction of Agra.

The Emperor Humayun, on reaching Agra, told Amir Saiyid Amiru-d din, that the Afghans had not defeated his army, but that he had seen supernatural beings fighting his soldiers, and turning back their horses. When he arrived at Sirhind, he told the same story to Muhibu-d din Sirhindi. When Sher Shah approached Agra,[60] the Emperor, unable to remain there, fled towards Lahore. Sher Shah was greatly displeased at this, and reproached Barmazid very much, and on his arrival at Agra remained there for some days himself, but sent Khawas Khan and Barmazid Gur in the direction of Lahore, with a large Afghan force, to pursue the Emperor.[61] On arriving at Dehli, the principal men and inhabitants of the city of Sambhal came and complained that Nasir Khan had oppressed and tyrannized over them in various ways.

[59] All the copies and many writers of the same period concur in reading Gwalir (which may also be read Gwaliyar).

[60] The *Tarikh-i Khan Jahan* (MS., p. 194) says he was two years arranging preliminaries and trying his forces before he advanced on Agra.

[61] The *Tarikh-i-Daudi* (MS., p. 230) says the instructions were to remain fifty *kos* in the rear of the Mughals, as Sher Shah only wished to expel them from Hindustan without coming to action.

Sher Shah said to Kutb Khan, "We must select some person endowed both with valour and justice whom to send to Sambhal, for in that *sarkar* are many lawless and rebellious persons, and the person selected should be able to keep them under." Kutb Khan replied, "That for these qualities there was no Afghan like to 'Isa Khan Kalkapur." Sher Khan replied, "Right, it shall be so. You yourself go to Masnad Ali 'Isa Khan, and tell him, if he consents, I will appoint him." Kutb Khan went to Isa Khan, who readily assented. . . . .

In addition to *sarkar* Sambhal, Sher Shah gave him the *parganas* of Kant and Gola for his family, and ordered him to maintain five thousand horse, and placed also Nasir Khan under him. When Sher Shah dismissed Isa Khan to go to *sarkar* Sambhal he said, "I am now at my ease regarding the whole country from Dehli to Lucknow." Masnad Ali, on his arrival at Sambhal, found Nasir Khan had seized Bairam Beg, the keeper of the seals to the Emperor, who afterwards in the time of the Emperor Akbar received the title of Khan-khanan. The reason of Bairam Beg being in Sambhal was as follows. When the army of the Emperor Humayun was dispersed, Bairam Beg went to Sambhal, having formed an intimate friendship with Mian Abdu-l Wahab, son of Mian Azizu-lla Danishmand, one of the chief men of the city of Sambhal. 'Abdu-l Wahab, from fear of Nasir Khan, dared not keep him in the city, but made him over to the Raja of Lukhnor,[62] by name Mitr Sen. The Raja kept

[62] All the copies and corresponding passages in other works concur in reading "Lakhnau;" but I suspect "Lakhnor" is meant—an ancient native capital of the Katharya Rajputs, a little to the east of Sambhal, on the banks of the Ramganga. More will be found respecting the place in my *Supplemental Glossary* (vol. ii., p. 136). It is observable that Dr. Dorn occasionally reads *Lucknor* where he should have said *Lucknow*. In this particular passage he is correct in reading *Lucknor.—Hist., Afghans.* p. 128.

him for some time in the northern part of his country, where there is much jungle. Nasir Khan was informed that Bairam Beg was with Mitr Sen, so he wrote to the Raja that he must bring Bairam Beg to him. The Raja, from fear and dread of Sher Shah, surrendered him to Nasir Khan, who was desirous of putting him to death. An old friendship had subsisted between Abdu-l Wahab and 'Isa Khan, from the time of Sultan Sikandar, so he went to 'Isa Khan, and told him he ought to save Bairam Beg from the hands of the cruel Nasir Khan, who was desirous of putting him to death. 'Isa Khan accordingly having rescued Bairam Beg from Nasir Khan, brought him into his own house, and kept him there for some time, and gave him an allowance for his support; and he took Raja Mitr Sen's security that whenever he ('Isa Khan) should go to Sher Shah, thither Bairam Beg should accompany him.

When 'Isa Khan joined Sher Shah, during the campaign of Mandu and Ujjain, he brought Bairam with him, and introduced him to Sher Shah in the town of Ujjain. Sher Shah angrily asked where he had been up to that time. Masnad Ali said he had been in the house of Shaikh Malhi Kahal. Sher Shah replied, "Since it is an established custom among the Afghans that whatever criminal takes refuge among the relatives of Shaikh Malhi Kahal should be pardoned, I also pardon Bairam Beg. When Sher Shah was about to leave the *darbar,* 'Isa Khan said: "You have for Shaikh Malhi's sake given Bairam Beg his life; give him also for my sake, who have brought him to you, a dress of honour and a horse, and order that he shall pitch his tent with Muhammad Kasim, who surrendered the fort of Gwalior. Sher Shah assigned him a place near Muhammad Kasim, when Sher Khan marched from Ujjain; but both Bairam Beg and Muhammad Kasim fled towards Gujarat. Muhammad Kasim was killed by the way, but Bairam Beg reached Gujarat. One Shaikh Gadai was in Gujarat, to whom he did good service, and from Gujarat, Bairam Beg reached the Emperor Humayun.

After the death of that Emperor, Bairam Beg, who had been dignified with the title of Khan-khanan, returned the kindness of Shaikh Gadai, Shaikh Abdu-l Wahab, and Raja Mitr Sen with every imaginable favour. 'Isa Khan was still alive; his age then was ninety years. Many persons said to him that he ought to wait on the Khan-khanan. Masnad Ali said: "I will not for any worldly gain wait on the Mughal, nor is it the custom of the sons of Masnad Ali Umar Khan to ask for a return of their favours." I have heard from Maulana Muhammad Binor and Abdu-l Momin, his son-in-law, who were among the intimates of the Khan-khanan, that they asked the Khan-khanan thus: "Did Masnad Ali 'Isa Khan ever do you a kindness?" He replied: "He saved my life: if he will come to me, I shall feel myself honoured. If I cannot give him more than Sher Shah, I at least will give him his own Sambhal." I, 'Abbas Khan, the author of the *Tuhfa-i Akbar Shahi,* and Masnad Ali 'Isa Khan Kalkapur came of the same tribe and family, and I am married to the daughter of his brother's son, whose name is Muzaffar Khan. Much of the history of the Afghans which I described I learnt from Khan-'azam Muzaffar Khan, whose ancestors were formerly nobles of Hindustan. When Sultan Sikandar banished Haibat Khan, the father of 'Isa Khan, the latter went to Sultan Mahmud, the King of Mandu, and became his chosen counsellor and associate; and when he left Sultan Mahmud and went to Muzaffar King of Gujarat, he also became his counsellor and friend.

When the Sultan took the fort of Mandu from the unbelievers, he said to Masnad Ali: "Go to Sultan Muzaffar, and tell him he should visit the fort of Mandu, for it is a fine place." Sultan Muzaffar said, "May the fort of Mandu bring Sultan Mahmud good fortune, for he is the master of it. I, for the sake of the Lord, came to his assistance. On Friday I will go up to the fortress, and having read the *khutba* in his name, will return," 'Isa Khan brought this good news to Sultan Mahmud. Afterwards, when he left Gujarat, and went to Sultan Ibrahim, he became also his associate and adviser. Sultan Ibrahim entrusted the city of Dehli to him, when Sultan Alau-d din, son of Sultan Bahlol, was repulsed from it; for in spite of all his efforts, 'Isa Khan wuld not surrender it. He afterwards went to Sher Shah, became one of his attendant nobles, and after he had conquered Dehli, Sher Shah gave Sambhal to him, as has before been stated. Sher Shah, entrusting Mewat to Haji Khan, went himself towards Lahore. On arriving near Sirhind, he bestowed it on Khawas Khan. Khawas Khan entrusted it to Malik Bhagwant, who was his slave. When the Emperor Humayun reached Lahore, certain Mughals, who had newly arrived from their own country, and had never yet encountered the Afghans, said to the Emperor, "You should send us to fight the Afghans," and vaunted much, saying, "Who and what manner of men are these Afghans, that they should be able to contend with us in the day of battle?" So the Emperor Humayun sent these Mughals to make the attempt, and Khawas Khan and Barmazid Gur, who had marched in advance of Sher Shah from Dehli, met them at Sultanpur, where they engaged. The Mughals were defeated, and retired to Lahore. Khawas Khan halted at Sultanpur; but the Emperor and Mirza Kamran quitted Lahore, which was shortly afterwards occupied by Sher Shah, who, however, made no halt there. On the third march beyond Lahore, he heard that Mirza Kamran had gone by way of the Judh Hills to Kabul, and that the Emperor Humayun was marching along the banks of the Indus to Multan and Bhakkar. The King went to Khushab, and thence despatched Kutb Khan Banet, Khawas Khan, Haji Khan, Habib Khan, Sarmast Khan, Jalal Khan Jaloi, 'Isa Khan Niazi Barmazid Gur, and the greater part of his army, in pursuit of the Emperor, towards Multan. He instructed them not to engage the Emperor, but to drive him beyond the borders of the kingdom and then to return. When they had gone two marches, they heard that the Mughal army had divided into two portions. The Afghan army was in great anxiety, lest, as the force with the King was so small, the Mughals should make forced marches, and attack him. The Afghan army, therefore, also dividing itself into two divisions, the one under Khawas Khan, 'Isa Khan, and others, crossed the river, and marched along the bank of the Jelam towards Multan; and Kutb Khan and the rest remained and marched along the nearer bank of the same stream. The Mughal division which had quitted the Emperor, and was marching towards Kabul, encountered Khawas Khan, and not being strong enough to fight, fled, leaving their drums and standards behind, which fell into Khawas Khan's hands,[63] and the Afghan army returning from that place, rejoined Sher Shah. Sher Shah delayed some time at Khushab. While there, Ismail Khan, and Ghazi Khan Biluchi, came and waited on him. Sher Shah ordered the Biluchis to brand their horses. Ismail Khan said: "Other persons brand their horses—I will brand my own body. Sher Shah was pleased and excused him from the branding, and confirmed to him the country of Sind. The chiefs of every tribe and family of Roh came to wait on Sher Shah. The writer's grandfather, Shaikh Bayazid Kalkapur Sarwani, who was the successor to the very holy Shaikh Ahmad Sarwani, who was the grandfather of Shaikh Malhi Kayal, whose holiness and glory is famous all over the country of Roh, and whose disciples and followers most of the Afghans are, and whose

[63] *The Tarikh-i Daudi,* which is partial to the fabulous, represents (MS., p. 235) that Khawas Khan came up with Humayun near Khushab, when the Emperor, being hard up for supplies, sent to him for something to eat, which he readily furnished; upon which the Emperor went on towards Thatta.

descendants are celebrated for their austerity and for the strictness of their devotional observances, and who are also known for their gallantry and wealth; nor does any person excel them in honour and consideration—the whole race of Afghans acknowledge their greatness, and their own, and their ancestors' virtues: this said Shaikh Bayazid came to Sher Shah at Khushab, and had an interview with him.

Since the previous kings of whom I have treated in this history paid extreme respect to Shaikh Bayazid, he was very anxious as to whether Sher Shah would or would not show him the same civilities. The moment Shaikh Bayazid came unto Sher Shah's *darbar,* the latter came forward several steps to receive him; and abasing himself gave Shaikh Bayazid precedence. My grandfather expected that Sher Shah would give him his hand, but he said: "Embrace me." When he took leave also, he showed every sign of respect and friendship. When he returned towards Bengal, Sher Shah sent him back to Roh, and gave him one *lac* of *tankas* in cash, as well as Bengal silks and clothes of Hindustan. The Shaikh said: "Since the time of the Langahs the Biluchis have possessed themselves of the rent-free tenures of my predecessors." Sher Shah ordered that Ismail Khan Biluch should receive instead the *pargana* of Ninduna, in the Ghakkar country, and that the Biluchis should be made to restore to Shaikh Bayazid, the rightful owner, the land of the Sarwanis, which they had usurped. Ismail Khan dared not disobey the orders of Sher Shah, so he took pargana Ninduna and the Ghakkar villages, and restored the Sarwanis' land to Shaikh Bayazid. Shaikh Bayazid came a second time to see Sher Shah during the Ujjain and Sarangpur campaign. . . . . Sher Shah conferred on the Shaikh 2000 bighas of land in the pargana of Batnur, which had been the settlement of his ancestors, and also fixed the amount of present he was to receive on visiting the king at a *lac* of *tankas,* and promised that after the fall of Kalinjar he would give him the provinces of Sind and Multan, the country of the Biluchis.

When Shaikh Bayazid surrendered his life to the Almighty, my father, Shaikh 'Ali, took his place in the country of Roh, and in those days he had an interview with Islam Khan, who also paid the customary respect and honour to Shaikh Ali without difference or diminution, and confirmed his assignments. In the reign of the Emperor Akbar I also enjoyed these as usual, until the twenty-fourth Ilahi year (corresponding to 987 A. H.), when the Emperor ordered that I should be advanced to the command of 500 horse, and brought to his presence. But the Kazi-'ali did not give a true account of myself or of my ancestors, but spoke ill of us and said, "Shaikh Abdu-l Nabi has given 2000 bighas of land to two Afghans!" In short, my bad fortune so ordered it that my share of the assignment (*madad-ma'ash*), was resumed. When the Khan-khanan, who was a follower of Saiyid Hamid, son of Saiyid Miran, son of Saiyid Mubarak of Bukhara and Gujarat, became acquainted with my history and that of my ancestors, he said it was a pity I should remain unemployed; but I refused employ, and said that I would go to the country of my fathers. He then brought Mir Hamid to my house without invitation, and since Mir Hamid was so kind as thus to honour me, I could not act in contravention to his wishes. So I entered the service of the chief of the great Shaikhs, Mir Saiyid Hamid. He assigned to me a clear 200 rupees a month, and moreover showed me all manner of kindness. At last, by ill luck of the unpropitious heavens, he sent me to Bajwara on some urgent business, and a short time afterwards was himself slain, at which I remained immersed in grief and distress.

Sher Shah gave to many of his kindred who came from Roh money and property far exceeding their expectations. . . . Sarang Ghakkar did not come to wait on Sher Shah. That monarch, therefore, marched with all his forces and retinue through all the hills of Padman and Garjhak, in order that he might choose a fitting site and build a fort there to keep down the Ghakkars, in which he might leave a garrison on the Kabul road,[64] when he himself returned. Having selected Rohtas, he built there the fort which now exists, and laid waste the country of the Ghakkars,[65] and carried them into captivity, and having seized the daughter of Sarang Ghakkar, bestowed her on Khawas Khan.

In the midst of this, news came from Bengal that Khizr Khan Bairak, the governor of Bengal, had married the daughter of Sultan Mahmud, late King of Bengal, and, after the manner of the kings of that country, sat on the "Toki," which means "an upper place." Sher Shah was much annoyed at this, and wishing to avert the evil ere it could take place, left Haibat Khan Niazi, Khawas Khan, 'Isa Khan Niazi, Habib Khan, Rai Hussain Jalwani, in the fort of Rohtas, and set out himself for Bengal. On his arrival in Bengal, Khizr Khan Bairak came to give him a regal reception. Sher Shah said to him: "Why did you without my order take in marriage the daughter of Sultan Mahmud, and seat yourself on the "Toki," after the manner of the kings of Bengal? It becomes not a noble of the State to do a single act without the King's permission. Sher Khan ordered him to receive a severe punshiment and to be put in chains, and said, that if any of his nobles should do anything without his leave, he should receive a similar punishment. And he divided the kingdom of Bengal into different provinces, and made Kazi Fazilat, better known as Kazi Fazihat, manager (*amir*) of Bengal, and himself returned to Agra.

[64] The *Tarikh-i-Khan Jahan* speaks of it (MS. p. 176) as being built on the boundary of Hindustan and Kabul.

[65] Some further details will be found lower down, and in the extracts from the *Makhzan-i Afghani.*

When he arrived at Agra, a letter arrived from Shuja'at Khan, saying that Muhammad Kasim had consented to the following terms: that the Afghans should be allowed to enter the fort ; that the Mughals should have free access to the camp of Sher Shah; and that as soon as Sher Shah should come to Gwalior, Muhammad Kasim was to be introduced to the king's presence, when he would give up the fort to the king's commissioners. Sher Shah replied that his standards would shortly move towards the country of Mandu, by way of Gwalior, in order to wreak on the rulers of Mandu his revenge for their backwardness in assisting Kutb Khan. At this time there were persons in the kingdom of Mandu who ruled independently. Mallu Khan, who had assumed the title of king, and the name of Kadir Shah, held possession and rule of the city of Shadmabad, that is to say the fort of Mandu, and of Ujjain, Sarangpur, and the fort of Rantambhor; secondly, Sikandar Khan Miana, who was ruler of the country of Sewas and Hindia; thirdly, Raja Partab Shah, the son of Bhupat Shah, son of Salahu-d din, who was a minor, and whose deputy Bhaia Puran Mal held the districts of Chanderi and Raisin; and, fourthly, Bhopal, who possessed the country of Bijagarh and Tamha.[66] When the king came to Gwalior,[67] Muhammad Kasim, who was one of Humayun's nobles, and governor of the fort, came and paid his respects to the king, and surrendered the fort to the royal commissioners. When he came to Gagrun, Shuja'at Khan sent Ram Sah, Raja of Gwalior, to bring Puran Mal of Raisin to the king. Puran Mal wrote, saying he would come if Shuja'at Khan himself went to fetch him. So Shuja'at Khan went to the fort of Raisin, and brought Puran Mal with him to the king's presence. Upon his setting out, the wife

[66] (Var. "Mabhar.")

[67] The *Tarikh-i Khan Jahan* (MS., p. 178) says the advance to Gwalior and Malwa occurred in 949 A.H.

of Raja Puran Mal, by name Ratnavali, who was exceedingly beloved by him, sent to Shuja't Khan, saying, "I will then break my fast when I shall see Puran Mal again, and the whole time he is away I will sit on a bastion of the fort, and watch for his return." Shuja'at Khan sent to her to be of good cheer, for that Bhaia Puran Mal would return to her next day. Shuja'at brought Puran Mal to the king's presence, with 6000 horsemen, none of whom were forty years of age. Sher Shah instantly bestowed 100 horses and 100 splendid dresses of honour on Puran Mal, and allowed him to return. Bhaia Puran Mal left to serve the king his younger brother, whose name was Chatur Bhoj.

When the king arrived at Sarnagpur, the agent of Mallu Khan came and made his obeisance, and said that Mallu Khan was coming to meet the king. Sher Shah ordered Shuja'at Khan to go and receive him, and he went accordingly. Sher Shah came, seated himself outside his tents, and held an open *darbar*. Shuja'at Khan brought Mallu Khan to him, and he asked where Mallu Khan had pitched his camp. He replied: "I have come alone into your presence, my place is in your *darbar*. My hope is, I may be permitted to perform the office of a sweeper therein." Shuja'at Khan represented that Mallu Khan had brought 200 horsemen with him. Sher Shah ordered that a scarlet tent, a bed, a canopy, and other conveniences, as well as a handsome entertainment, should be provided for him. When they marched from Sarangpur, Sher Shah showed the whole array of his army to Mallu Khan, who was astounded, for he had never anywhere seen such an army before.[68] At every stage they

[68] The *Waki'at-i Mushtaki* (MS., p. 102) and the *Tarikh-i Daudi* (MS., p. 254) record an interesting military spectacle which astonished Mallu Khan at this review. When the royal umbrella came in sight, the cavalry drew their sabres, galloped forward towards the umbrella, dismounted from their horses, and saluted the king in due

threw up an earthen entrenchment, and when he saw the labour and exertions of the soldiers, and the rigour of Sher Shah's discipline, Mallu Khan said to the Afghans, "You submit yourselves to wonderful labours and exertions, night and day you have no rest; ease and comfort are things forbidden to you. "The afghans replied—"Such is our master's custom. . . . . It behoves a soldier, whatever service his chief may order, or whatever labour or exertion he may require, not to consider it a hardshsp. Ease is for women, it is shameful to honourable men."[69]

When Sher Shah went to Ujjain, he encamped at Kalidah. Sikandar Khan Miana came and made obei-

---

form, "as was their habit on the day of battle." Each division did this in succession.

[69] On one of the marches between Sarangpur and Ujjain, Sher Shah communicated some of the early events of his life to Mallu Khan, who was riding with him. He told him how he had laboured hard in his youth, and went every day on foot fifteen *kos* in pursuit of game, armed with his bow and arrows. On one of these excursions he fell in with a party of thieves and highwaymen, with whom he associated for some time, plundering the country all round; till one day, when seated in a boat with his new comrades, he was pursued "by his enemies," who, after a conflict, were completely victorious. Upon this, placing his bow and arrows on his head, he plunged into the water, and after swimming for three *kos* escaped with his life, and from that period abandoned his new profession. The *Waki-'at-i Mushtaki* (MS. p. 103) and the *Tarikh-i Daudi* (MS. p. 256). This is a novelty, and either Sher Shah was "chaffing" his guest, whom he previously vowed to avenge himself upon for his premeditated insult about the seal, and who appears from all his sayings and doings to have been a great simpleton; or our author has, as usual, given too ready credence to an improbable story. Abu-l Fazl, however, and other courtly Timurian authors, are very fond of representing that Sher Shah's early life was devoted to plunder and robbery and every kind of enormity.

sance. Sher Shah assigned the country of Mandu to Shuja'at Khan; and when he reflected that Mallu Khan had submitted to him, ... he pardoned him, and bestowed on him the *sarkar* of Kalpi.[70]

Mallu Khan, having brought his family out of Ujjain, considered that he was not equal to the labour and exertion which Sher Khan required, and that therefore it was better to escape by some contrivance from his camp.[71] Accordingly, like a Hindu slave, he made up his mind to run away. Sher Shah perceived his intention, and ordered Shuja'at Khan to arrest him. Shuja'at Khan looked towards Mallu Khan, who, being an intelligent man, understood what was going on, and said to Shuja'at Khan: "Tell the king that I have no carriage to take my family to Kalpi." When Shuja'at Khan represented this, it was ordered that 100 camels and 100 mules, with camelmen, and mulemen, and several carts with drivers, should be given to Mallu Khan for the conveyance of his family. When he received the camels, mules and carriages, he took them, together with their drivers, to his own encampment, and gave them some very powerful wine, so that they got drunk and became insensible. Mallu Khan, taking his treasures and his family, absconded. When it was day, it became known that Mallu Khan had fled. Sher Shah said: "Mallu Khan, the slave! Have you seen what a trick he has played me? . . . . Sher Shah was angry with Shuja'at Khan and sent him in pursuit of Mallu Khan, saying:

[70] The *Tarikh-i Khan Jahan* says "Marehra." The *Waki'at-i Mushtaki* and the *Tarikh-i Daudi* "Lakhnau".

[71] The *Waki'at-i Mushtaki* (MS. p. 104) and the *Tarikh-i Daudi* (MS. p. 257) say that he was inspired with alarm at seeing one day a party of respectable Mughals, who had been taken prisoners at Gwalior, working in the camp, as common labourers, at the circumvallation which was constructed every day, and that he apprehended the same fate awaited his own person.

"Wherever Mallu Khan may go, you go also and bring him to me. Did not I tell you to arrest him? But you did not, and acted negligently."[72] Shuja'at Khan went in pursuit, but failed to overtake Mallu Khan, who went to Sultan Mahmud at Gujarat,[73] and Shuja'at Khan returned from the frontier of Mandu. The whole of the kingdom of Mandu had been bestowed on Shuja'at Khan; but the king in his anger deprived him of it, and in lieu of it gave him Sewas, Hindia, etc. which had

[72] The *Waki'at-i Mushtaki* (MS., p. 104) and the *Tarikh-i Daudi* (MS., p. 259), on the contrary, say, that on Shuja'at Khan's representing that it was Mallu Khan's intention to fly, Sher Shah replied, that he was anxious he should effect his escape, and had therefore thrown every facility in his way for that purpose. This, however, is scarcely consistent with the hot pursuit "by soldiers without number," which immediately followed his departure. The same passage teaches us a bit of royal and patrician morality amongst these Afghans: "As he now," said Sher Shah, "intends to run away, say nothing to him, and pretend not to observe anything. If he offers you money in bribery, take it immediately, and let him run off. Shuja'at Khan consequently took from Mallu Kadir Shah 700,000 *tankas*, and let him go his way, and at night-time finding his opportunity, he took to flight." This shameless prostitution, with the encouragement of the Shah, is mentioned by Ahmad Yadgar (MS. p. 197), but the persons are different. "If that black-face offer you a bribe, take it without scruple and let him go; so Ahmad Khan Sur and Fath Khan Niazi, who were in charge of him, took 1000 pieces of red gold and let him escape."

[73] Ahmad Yadgar's account is different. He says (MS. pp. 197-8) that Mallu Khan plundered Sarangpur and other places, and was at last slain with all his adherents in a night attack by Haibat Khan, who on that occasion obtained his title of 'Azam Humayun; which our author, a little below, says was conferred for the conquest of Multan.

been in Sikandar Khan Miana's possession, equal to the maintenance of 4000 horse; and gave Ujjain to Darya Khan Gujarati, who had been wazir of Sultan Mahmud, King of Gujarat, and who had fled to Sher Shah; and Sarangpur to Alam Khan Ladi, who also had been noble of Sultan Mahmud's court; and making Haji Khan and Junaid Khan *faujdars* of that country, he left them in the city of Dhar, and returned himself, by the fort of Rantambhor,[74] on the road to which place Sikandar Khan Miana, who had been ruler of *sarkar* Sewas, fled. 'Usman Khan, whose name was previously Abu-l Farra, was governor of Rantambhor, on behalf of Mallu Khan. When Sher Shah approached, he came and submitted to him, and Sher Shah, making over the fort of Rantambhor to his eldest son 'Adil Khan, went himself to Agra.[75]

When Sher Shah left Mandu for Agra, Nasir Khan, brother of Sikandar Khan Miana, with 6000 horse and 200 elephants, came against Shuja'at Khan. Shuja'at Khan had with him only 2000 horse. Nasir Khan said to his men: "Seize Shuja'at Khan alive that I may retain him as a hostage for Sikandar Khan.[76] When Sher Shah releases Sikandar Khan, I will release Shuja'at Khan." When Shuja'at heard that Nasir Khan was approaching,

[74] (Here called "Ranthur.")

[75] Ahmad Yadgar (MS. pp. 292-5) mentions during this campaign an expedition against Chanderi, commanded by Walidad Khan Kakar, which was successful through the treachery of the Raja's nephew. Elephants, horses and treasure fell into the hands of the victors on the capture of Chanderi, and the Raja's beautiful daughter was sent to Sher Shah. The treacherous nephew gained his ends by being made Raja of Chanderi.

[76] From this it would appear either that Nasir Khan did not know of Sikandar Khan's flight, narrated above, or that the latter had been again seized.

he went out to meet him, and gave him battle at Nil-garh.[77] When the two armies were commingled together, part of Nasir Khan's and part of Shuja'at Khan's force were put to flight. Three men had sworn an oath to attack only Shuja'at Khan. One was Mian 'Umar, the second Saiyid Tahir, the third Koka. One of these wounded Shuja'at Khan in the neck with a dagger; the second wounded him in the nostril with a spear thrust, and broke his front teeth; the third, having wounded him with a sabre, caught hold of the hair of his head, to take him alive before Nasir Khan. Shuja'at Khan struck him with his sabre on the hand and cut it off, and so freed himself. Jajhar Khan who was of Shuja't Khan's own tribe, slew the second horsemen; and Mubarak Khan Shirini killed the third. So Shuja'at was rescued, and raised again his standard which had fallen. Those of Shuja'at Khan's men who had fled returned, and rallying round him on all sides, gained the victory. Nasir Khan fled and the 200 elephants fell into Shuja'at Khan's hands. Almighty God made Shuja'at Khan victorious, and he returned from Nilgarh to Hindia.

After this, Shuja'at Khan heard that Mallu Khan was approaching, and had surrounded Haji Khan, who had fortified himself in Mandu. Although Shuja'at's wounds were not well, yet taking the 200 elephants with him, he went to the succour of Haji Khan, and encamped outside the walls. The next day at sunrise the two armies, drawn out in battle array, engaged in the open field. The Afghan army displayed such gallantry as is beyond all power of description; the victory remained with Shuja'at Khan and Mallu Khan fled to Gujarat. When Sher Shah heard this intelligence, he called Haji Khan to his own presence from Mandu, and bestowed on him the command of 12000 horse, and gave to Shuja'at Khan Ujjain, Mandu Sarangpur, and Mansur in jagir;

[77] or "Mahalkarra."

and the country of Sewas he gave to Shams Khan, Bihar Khan, and Mir Khan Niazi, who were of Shuja'at Khan's kindred; and Shuja'at Khan became ruler of all the country of Mandu.

Sher Shah went from Agra in the direction of Bihar and Bengal,[78] when he was attacked by fever and ague. During his illness he several times said: "I did wrong when I said I would go towards Bengal. If Almighty God will vouchsafe me a recovery from this fever, I will return with all speed; and Puran Mal, who has enslaved the families of the Musulmans in Chanderi and has made dancing-girls of their daughters, and did not accompany my son Kutb Khan—him I will so punish that he may be a warning to others, that hereafter no unbelievers in Hind may oppress and injure the families of Musulmans.[79] Almighty God vouchsafed to Sher Shah a recovery from that fever, and he quickly turned back towards Agra. When he arrived there, in all the pride of his state, he set off for the country of Mandu, in the year A. H. 950.[80] and took the fort of Raisin. He ordered his noble son, Jalal Khan, to go on in advance with his victorious troops. When Jalal Khan came to the stage of Bhilsa, Sher Shah joined him. From this

[78] The *Tarikh-i Daudi* (MS., p. 264) says that after his return from Malwa, he remained two years at Agra, going intermediately to Dehli, before he went towards Bengal.

[79] Ahmad Yadgar (MS. pp. 296-9) represents them chiefly as captured from the families of the Saiyids of Bilgram. He also says that this occurred on his road to Raisin, and that before starting on this expedition he had been hunting in the neighbourhood of Sorin and Badaun.

[80] This expedition the *Tarikh-i-Khan Jahan* (MS. p. 180) also ascribes to the year 950. In that work Puran Mal is called the son of Rai Salhadi Purbiya, a Gehlot Rajput.

place Sher Shah, by forced marches, brought his conquering army into the vicinity of the fort of Raisin.[81] Bhaia Puran Mal sent 600 elephants, but did not himself come out. Sher Shah laid siege to Raisin, when a report came from Khawas Khan that enmity had broken out between him and Haibat Khan, and requesting him to send for a representative from each of them. When Sher Shah knew of the quarrel between Khawas Khan and Haibat Khan Niazi, he sent for 'Isa Khan and Habib Khan, and confirmed Haibat Khan in the Government of the Punjab, attaching Fath Jang Khan to him. And whereas Fath Khan Jat had been in rebellion in Kayula, and in the time of the Mughals had plundered the whole country and laid it waste as far as Panipat,[82] and the Biluchis had got into their power and possession the country of Multan, Sher Shah ordered Haibat Khan to expel these people from the country, and to punish them, and to restore to prosperity the city of Multan. Instantly on the receipt of this farman, Haibat Khan said to the Vakil of Chakar Rind, who at that time was Ruler of Satgarh, "Go, tell Chakar Rind that I shall halt within his confines, and he must have his forces ready, for I am going to seize Mahla." . . . .

Early in the morning news came that Haibat Khan had arrived. Chakar went out to welcome Haibat Khan,

[81] What follows until the resumption of the story of the capture of Raisin is only in one MS.

[82] The *Makhzan-i Afghani* (MS., p. 242) says, "Sher Shah ordered Haibat Khan to seize Fath Khan. This Fath Khan was of Kob Kabula (Kapura?), who had devasted the entire tract of Lakhi Jangal, and kept the high roads from Lahore to Dehli in a constant ferment." Then follows an incomprehensible passage, which has by no means been elucidated by Dr. Dorn's mode of translating it. The *Tarikh-i Khan Jahan Lodi* is unusually deficient in the corresponding passage, and does not help us in the least.—*Dorn,* p., 134.

but was in a state of great alarm. As soon as Haibat Khan saw him, he said "I shall take your muster at Dipalpur, lest in the delay Fath Khan should escape." Within two days Haibat Khan arrived at the Pattan[83] of Kutb 'Alam Shaikh Farid. Fath Khan fled and Haibat Khan pursued him. As Fath Khan had his family and women with him, he perceived he was unable to escape from Haibat Khan. There was near Karor and Fathpur a mud fort; he took possession of it, and Haibat Khan coming up in pursuit, laid siege to it. Fath Khan held out the fort for some days; at last, being reduced to extremities, he sent Shaikh Ibrahim, son of Kutb Alam Shaikh Farid, to Haibat Khan as an intercessor. He came before Haibat Khan, who said to him, "I am a servant of Sher Shah's, what my master orders that I must do." He put Fath Khan in prison. In the night, Hindu Biluch with 300 men came out of the mud fort, and attacking the besiegers fiercely, cut their way through by their valour. When it was day, the Afghans occupied the fort. The women of the better sort had been mostly slain by the Biluchis, and the rest the Afghans made slaves; and they took Hindu Biluch and Bakshu Langah prisoners. Haibat Khan then went to the city of Multan, which the Biluchis had laid waste. Haibat Khan restored it to its former state, and the inhabitants who were scattered abroad he again collected together, and he wrote letters to Sher Shah reporting the true condition of the country, and concerning the capture of Fath Khan, Hindu Biluch, and Bakshu Langah. Sher Shah was exceedingly rejoiced, and made him a Masnad Ali and gave him the title of Azam Humayun. He also gave him a red tent, and wrote to him to repeople Multan and to observe the customs of the Langahs, and not to measure the land, but take a

[83] Pak-pattan.

share of the produce.[84] He ordered him to put Fath Khan and Hindu Biluch to death, to keep Bakshu Langah or his son always with him, but to confirm his districts to him. As soon as 'Azam Humayun received this order at Multan, he left Fath Jang Khan in Multan and came to Lahore, and put Fath Khan and Hindu Biluch to death. Fath Jang Khan so repeopled Multan, and showed such benevolence to the people, that Multan flourished more than it had done, even under the Langahs, and in the country of Multan he founded a city which he called "Shergarh." Sher Shah, while besieging the fort of Raisin, gave orders that no Afghan should approach it; for that he would take the fort by the exercise of his skill and prudence.

One day, certain followers and retainers of the Afghans were sitting together, when the conversation turned on the gallantry and valour of Bhaia Puran Mal's soldiers. Most of those present said, that no one in those days was a match for Puran Mal's soldiers in these qualities, who daily came out of the fort and said: "There is no one in the army of Sher Khan who can fight with us,' and that it was from fear that none of the Afghans approached them. When the Afghans amongst these retainers pondered on these remarks, the reproach thus thrown upon Afghan honour overcame them, and they said, "Though Sher Shah should cut our throats or banish us from his kingdom, yet we will for once encounter the soldiers of Puran Mal, that we may test their gallantry and valour."

The next day before sunrise, 1500 horsemen assembled at an appointed place, and drawing up in order of battle, sent to Puran Mal, saying: "Your men every day

[84] *jarib nakunad wa hissa az ghilla bagirad.* The *Makhzan-i Afghani* says that orders were issued to take only a fourth of the produce of grain for the government share.

boast of their valour. We, 1500 horse, against Sher Shah's command, have come and are drawn up in order of battle; do you also collect your men, and come out of the fort, that we may fight, and the valour of either side may be made manifest." Bhaia Puran Mal had great reliance on the valour and gallantry of his men, and did not think the Afghans were at all equal to them in bravery. He sent out to answer the challenge the most famous of his soldiers, veterans in battle, and he himself took his seat above the gateway. The Afghans and Rajputs joined battle, and the fight continued till the first watch of the day, up to which time neither party had succeeded in driving the other from their ground. At length the Afghans got the advantage, and began to make the Rajputs give ground, when such bravery was displayed on both sides as surpasses all description. In the end, Almighty God gave the victory to the Afghans, and they drove the Rajputs from their position to near the gate of the fort. The Rajputs again made a stand near the gate of the fort, but the Afghans made a headlong charge upon them, which they were unable to resist, and fled within the gate: and the Afghans returned triumphant to their camp.

When Sher Shah heard that the Arghan retainers had displayed such gallantry and bravery, he was much pleased; but in public severely reprimanded those who had risked an engagement in defiance of his orders. After some days, he gave fitting rewards to every one of them, and good appointments and *jagirs*, and said, "The gallantry you have displayed has been made known to me; now look at my work and see what I shall do to this fort." After this Sher Shah issued an order that they should bring all the brass in camp and make mortars (*degha*) of it. When, according to his order, they had brought all the brass that was in the bazar or in the tents of the soldiery, in pots, dishes, and pans, they made it all into mortars, and when they were finished he ordered them to bombard the fort from all simultaneously. When they had battered the fort and breached it in all directions, Puran Mal became alarmed, and after the lapse of six months, he came out himself to Sher Shah, who said to him, "I grant you quarter, and the government of Benares; provided you give up the families of the Musulmans whom you have enslaved." Puran Mal replied: "I had none of these families in slavery, neither am I the Raja; I am but his deputy. I will go to him, and I will say whatever you order me, and see what he replies." Sher Khan permitted him to go. When he went up into the fort, he got together all his jewels, and sent to Sher Khan to say, "I dare not again face your presence, but do you first go away two marches from the fort. I will come out and give up the fort to your soldiers, and go myself to other countries. And if your eldest son 'Adil Khan and Kutb Khan Banet will bind themselves by promise and oaths that I shall suffer no injury in property or person, I will come with my women and family out of the fort." Sher Shah told 'Adil Khan and Kutb Khan Banet what Puran Mal said, and ordered them to satisfy him and bring him out. Kutb Khan Banet went up to the fort, and binding him self by solemn oaths, brought Puran Mal out of the fort of Raisin with his family and wives. Kutb Khan requested that some encamping ground for Puran Mal might be selected, and Sher Shah indicated a spot in the midst of his encampment, and Kutb Khan himself accompanied Puran Mal to the spot Sher Shah had directed.

After some days the widows of the chief men of Chanderi and others waited for Sher Shah by the roadside, and cried out to him. Sher Shah asked who they were, and ordered them to be brought to him. They said: "We have suffered from this inhuman and malignant infidel all kinds of tyranny and oppression. He has slain our husbands, and our daughters he has enslaved, and has made dancing-girls of them, and has seized our lands, and all our worldly goods, for a long time past. . . If you do not give us justice, hereafter, in the day of resurrection, when the first and the last of all men shall be collected together, we will accuse you." As Sher Shah was a believing and just ruler, on hearing these zeal-stirring words of the oppressed, the tears dropped from his eyes, and he said: "Have patience, for I have brought him out by promises and oaths." They replied: "Consult with your *'Ulama,* and act upon the decision they shall pronounce." When Sher Shah came back to his tent, he sent for all of the *'Ulama* who accompanied his victorious army, and related one by one the inhuman deeds Puran Mal had committed with respect to the wives and families of the Musulmans, and asked them to give their decision. Amir Shaikh Rafi'u-d din and the other *'Ulama* who accompanied the victorious army pronounced a decision for the death of Puran Mal.

At night orders were given to 'Isa Khan Hajib, that he should desire his troops to collect with the elephants in all haste at a certain spot, for that Sher Shah intended to make a forced march towards Gondwana. To Habib Khan he gave secret orders that he should watch Bhaia Puran Mal, and take care he did not fly, and not to speak of a word of this to any living creature, for that he (Sher Shah) had long entertained this design. When the elephants and troops were at the appointed spot, they reported it. Sher Shah ordered that at sunrise they should surround the tents of Bhaia Puran Mal. Puran Mal was told that they were surrounding his encampment, and going into the tent of his beloved wife Ratnavali, who sang Hindi melodies very sweetly, he cut off her head, and coming out said to his companions: "I have done this: do you also slay your wives and families." While the Hindus were employed in putting their women and families to death, the Afghans on all sides commenced the slaughter of the Hindus. Puran Mal and his companions, like hogs at bay, failed not to exhibit valour and gallantry, but in the twinkling of an eye all were slain. Such of their wives and families as were not slain were captured. One daughter of Puran Mal and three sons of his elder brother were taken alive, the rest were all killed. Sher Khan gave the daughter of Puran Mal to some itinerant minstrels (*bazigaran*), that they might make her dance in the bazars, and ordered the boys to be castrated, that the race of the oppressor might not increase. He made over the fort of Raisin to Munshi Shahbaz Khan Acha-khail Sarwani, and returned himself towards Agra, and remained at the capital during the rainy season.[85]

After the conclusion of the rains, he consulted his nobles of name, and the wise among his courtiers, saying that he was quite at ease concerning the kingdom of Hind. . . . The nobles and chiefs said, ". . . . It seems expedient that the victorious standards should move towards the Dekhin, for certain rebellious slaves have got the country out of the power of their master, and have revolted, and following the heresy of the people of dissent (*Shia*), abuse the holy posterity. It is incumbent

[85] Ahmad Yadgar (MS., p. 304) says that before Sher Shah's return to Agra, the Shaikh-zadas of Barnawa represented that their country had been plundered, and their wives and daughters carried off by Basdeo, a Rajput. Duda Miana was sent to chastise him which he did so effectually that the captives were all released, and immense plunder accrued to the victors. This is followed by another expedition against some Rajkunwar Rajputs, but the author's notions are so lax on geography, that it is quite impossible to fix the locality of either affair. The former, though with some variation in the details, is the same as that which was instigated by the Shaikh-zadas of Bhandner, as recorded in the *Waki'at-i Mushtaki* (MS., p. 109).

on the powerful and fortunate to root out this innovating schism from the Dekhin." Sher Shah replied: "What you have said is most right and proper, but it has come into my mind that since the time of Sultan Ibrahim, the infidel *zamindars* have rendered the country of Islam full of unbelievers, and have thrown down the *masjids* and buildings of the believers and placed idol-shrines in them, and they are in possession of the country of Dehli and Malwa. Until I have cleansed the country from the existing contamination of the unbelievers, I will not go into any other country. . . . First, I will root out that accursed infidel Maldeo, for that he was the servant of the ruler of Nagor and Ajmir, who placed the greatest confidence in him. The evil-minded and ungrateful infidel slew his master, and by violence and oppression possessed himself of those kingdom." The chiefs and nobles assented, and it was so settled. In the year 950 A.H. (1543-4 A.D.).[86] the king ordered that his conquering forces, beyond all calculation or numeration, should, under the shadow of his victorious standards, march towards the country of Nagor, Ajmir, and Judhpur. I have heard from the mouth of the respectably descended Shaikh Muhammad, and of the Khan-'azam, and of Muzaffar Khan, that in this campaign Sher Shah had so great an army with him that the best calculators, in spite of all reflection and thought and cal-

[86] Elphinstone (His. India. vol. ii., p. 149) says 951 H.; but as 950 H. began in April 1543, Sher Shah might easily have completed the conquest of Raisin in the hot months, returned to Agra for the rainy season, and set out for Marwar with the six best months of 950 H. before him. If he deferred his Marwar expedition to the cold season of 951 H., there would be no time for his subsequent return to Agra and operations against Chitor and Kalinjar. The latter alone, according to the *Waki'at-i Mushtaki* (MS., p. 110), and the *Tarikh-i Daudi* (MS., p. 285), occupied eight months.

culation were at a loss to number and reckon them, and we often ascended the tops of eminences that the length and breadth of the army might appear to us; but so exceeding was its magnitude, that its whole length and breadth were never visible together; and we asked old men of great age, whether they had ever seen or heard of so great an army, but they replied they had not.[87]

When Sher Shah marched from the capital of Agra, and arrived at Fathpur Sikri, he ordered that each division of the army should march together in order of battle, and should throw up an earthen entrenchment at every halting-ground. On the way they encamped one day on a plain of sand, and in spite of every labour, they could not, on account of the sand, make an entrenchment. Sher Shah considered by what contrivance the entrenchment could be completed. Muhmud Khan, grandson[88] of Sher Shah, said: "Let my lord order that sacks should be filled with sand, and that they should make the entrenchment with the bags." Sher Shah praised his grandson's contrivance, and was greatly delighted, and ordered that they should make the fortification of bags filled with sand, and, accordingly, at that halting place they did so. When he approached the enemy, Sher Khan contrived a

[87] The host of the Rajputs could have been scarcely less, if we are to believe the extravagant statement of the *Makhzan-i-Afghani*, which (MS., p. 249) sets it down at 50,000 cavalry and 300,000 infantry. The *Tarikh-i-Khan Jahan* (MS., p. 182) modestly retrenches the 300,000 infantry altogether.

[88] One copy reads "son", but he was "grandson", being, according to the *Makhzan-i-Afghani* (MS., p. 250) the son of Adil Khan. Dorn (p. 138) calls him "nephew". The *Tarikh-i-Khan Jahan* (MS., p. 182) makes out that he was a grandchild by a daughter, and only seven years old when he suggested this sagacious advice. It does not mention the name of this precocious child.

stratagem; and having written letters in the name of Maldeo's nobles to this effect, viz., "Let not the king permit any anxiety or doubt to find its way to his heart. During the battle we will seize Maldeo, and bring him to you," and having inclosed these letters in a *kharita* or silken bag, he gave it to a certain person, and directed him to go near to the tent of the *vakil* of Maldeo, and remain there, and when he went out to drop the *kharita* on his way, and conceal himself. Sher Shah's agent did as he was ordered; and when the *vakil* of Maldeo saw the *kharita* lying, he picked it up, and sent the letters to Maldeo. When the latter learnt their contents, he was much alarmed, and fled without fighting. Although his nobles took oaths of fidelity, he did not heed them. Some of the chieftains, such as Jaya Chandel and Goha, and others, came and attacked Sher Shah, and displayed exceeding valour. Part of the army was routed, and a certain Afghan came to Sher Shah, and abused him in his native tongue, saying "Mount, for the infidels are routing your army." Sher Shah was performing his morning devotions, and was reading the *Musta'-abi-i 'ashr*. He gave no reply to the Afghan. By a sign he ordered his horse and mounted, when news of victory was brought, to the effect that Khawas Khan had slain Jaya and Goha with all their forces. When Sher Shah learnt the valour and gallantry of Jaya and Goha, he said: "I had nearly given the kingdom of Dehli for a millet (*bajra*) seed."[89] He left Khawas Khan and 'Isa Khan Niazi, and some other chiefs, in the country of Nagor, and himself returned. Khawas Khan founded a city in his own name near the fort of Judhpur, and called it "Khawaspur," and brought into his power and possession the whole country of Nagor and Ajmir, the fort of Judhpur, and the districts of Marwar. Maldeo went to the fort of Siwana, on the borders of Gujarat.

[89] An allusion to the barrenness of Marwar.

Sher Shah's nobles represented to him that, as the rainy season was near at hand, it was advisable to go into cantonments. Sher Shah replied, "I will spend the rainy season in a place where I can carry on my work," and marched towards the fort of Chitor.[90] When he was yet twelve *kos* from the fort of Chitor, the Raja who was its ruler sent him the keys. When Sher Shah came to Chitor, he left in it the younger brother of Khawas Khan, Mian Ahmad Sarwani, and Husain Khan Khilji. Sher Shah himself marched towards Kachwara. His eldest son 'Adil Khan took leave to go and visit Rantambhor. Sher Shah said: "I give you leave in order to please you, but come again quickly, and do not remain for a long time at that fort." When Sher Shah came near Kachwara, Shuja'at Khan went towards Hindia. Certain persons who were envious of Shuja'at Khan, said that Shuja'at Khan kept up no troops, though he had to maintain 12,000 horse, and on this account he dared not come into the presence, and made a pretext of going to Hindia. The sons of Shuja'at Khan, Mian Bayazid, and Daulat Khan, were with Sher Shah, and wrote the true state of the case to Shuja'at Khan. On hearing the news, Shuja'at Khan came to Kachwara, to the king, and requested his horses should be branded. 7500 he passed under the brand, and he said that the rest were in his

[90] This makes it evident that he could scarcely have remained at all at Agra on his return at the close of 950 or beginning of 951 H. Indeed, had not the *Tarikh-i Daudi*, (MS., p. 284) mentioned his proceedings at Ajmir. and his visit to the shrine of Khwaja Mu'inu-d din Chishti, his return to Agra at all might have been disputed. Shortly after the beginning of 951 H. he must have started for Chitor, marching during the hot weather, passing the rains in Kachwara, and then occupying the closing months of 952 and the beginning of 953 with the siege of Kalinjar. This makes the chronology very plain.

districts on duty, and if ordered he would send for them and pass them too under the brand. Sher Shah replied: "There is no necessity for branding them, for your force is with you; and as to the persons who have defamed you, their faces are blackened." When he dismissed Shuja'at Khan, he said: "As soon as you receive news that Kalinjar[91] has fallen, do you, without fail, set off for the Dekhin with all haste. Do not delay or linger at all."

Sher Shah himself marched from Kachwara towards Kalinjar. When he reached the stage of Shahbandi, news came that 'Alam Khan Miana had created a disturbance in the Doab, and having raised the province of Mirath (Meerut), had ravaged great part of the neighbouring country. Sher Shah turned from Shahbandi, and had gone two marches, when news arrived that Alam Khan had been conquered; for Bhagwant, the slave of Khawas Khan, and governor of Sirhind, had slain him near Sirhind. Upon this, Sher Shah turned again towards Kalinjar.[92] The Raja of Kalinjar, Kirat Singh, did not come out to meet him. So he ordered the fort to be invested, and threw up mounds against it, and in a short time the mounds rose so high that they overtopped the fort. The men who were in the streets and houses were exposed and the Afghans shot them with their arrows and muskets from off the mounds. The cause of this tedious mode of capturing the fort was this. Among the women of Raja Kirat Singh was a Patar slave-girl, that is a dancing girl. The king had

[91] So spelt in all the copies. It is more usual to write it "Kâlinjar."

[92] Ahmad Yadgar (MS., p. 313) says that the reason for his advancing against Kalinjar was, that Birsingdeo Bundela, who had been summoned to Court, had fled and taken refuge with the Raja of Kalinjar, who refused to give him up.

heard exceeding praise of her, and he considered how to get possession of her, for he feared lest if he stormed the fort, the Raja Kirat Singh would certainly make a *jauhar,* and would burn the girl.

On Friday, the 9th of Rabi'u-l awwal, 952 A.H., when one watch and two hours of the day was over, Sher Shah called for his breakfast, and eat with his *'ulama* and priests, without whom he never breakfasted. In the midst of breakfast, Shaikh Nizam said, "There is nothing equal to a religious war against the infidels. If you be slain you become a martyr, if you live you become a *ghazi*. When Sher Shah had finished eating his breakfast, he ordered Darya Khan to bring loaded shells,[93] and went up to the top of a mound, and with his own hand shot off many arrows, and said, "Darya Khan comes not; he delays very long." But when they were at last brought, Sher Shah came down from the mound, and stood where they were placed. While the men were employed in discharging them, by the will of God Almighty, one shell full of gunpowder struck on the gate of the fort and broke, and came and fell where a great number of other shells were placed. Those which were

[93] Perhaps this may mean only "rockets." The words are "*hukkaha pur az atish*". It is to be remarked that there is no mention of *deg,* a mortar; and the shape of a *hukka,* or smoking-bowl, is not unlike that of a loaded rocket. Moreover, if a shell had burst, except very close, it would not have ignited other shells, and shells do not usually *rebound* unexploded; whereas, it is a common occurrence for a rocket to retrace its path, especially, as appears here to have been the case, when the stick breaks. On the other hand, it is to be remembered that the shape of a *hukka* is still more like a shell; and that there is, and was, a specific word for rocket (*ban*)—a Hindi vocable in common use even in Persian authors, and which might easily have been introduced in this passage without any violation of usage or propriety.

loaded all began to explode. Shaikh Halil, Shaikh Nizam, and other learned men, and most of the others escaped and were not burnt, but they brought out Sher Shah partially burnt. A young princess who was standing by the rocket was burnt to death. When Sher Shah was carried into his tent, all his nobles assembled in darbar; and he sent for 'Isa Khan Hajib, and Masnad Khan Kalkapur, son-in-law of 'Isa Khan, and the paternal uncle of the author, to come into his tent, and ordered them to take the fort while he was yet alive. When 'Isa Khan came out and told the chiefs that it was Sher Shah's order that they should attack on every side and capture the fort, men came and swarmed out instantly on every side like ants and locusts; and by the time of afternoon prayers captured the fort, putting every one to the sword, and sending all the infidels to hell. About the hour of evening prayers, the intelligence of the victory reached Sher Shah, and marks of joy and pleasure appeared on his countenance. Raja Kirat Singh, with seventy men, remained in a house. Kutb Khan the whole night long watched the house in person lest the Raja should escape. Sher Shah said to his sons that none of his nobles need watch the house, so that the Raja escaped out of the house and the labour and trouble of this long watching was lost. The next day at sunrise, however, they took the Raja alive.[91]

On the 10th Rabi-'u-l Awwal, 952 A.H. (May, 1545 A.D.) Sher Shah went from the hostel of this world to rest in the mansion of happiness, and ascended peacefully from the abode of this world to the lofty heavens. The date was discovered in the words *az atash murd*, "He died from fire."

[91] The *Makhzan-i Afghani* says that the first act of Islam Shah's reign was to order him for execution.

CONCLUSION OF THE WORK

On certain matters regarding Sher Shah, on which he was busied day and night and which he enjoined to his sons, chiefs and nobles, and which he caused to be recorded.

When fortune gave into the hands of Sher Shah the bridle of power, and the kingdom of Hind fell under his dominion, he made certain laws, both from his own ideas, and by extracting them from the works of the learned, for securing relief from tyranny, and for the repression of crime and villainy; for maintaining the prosperity of his realms, the safety of the highways, and the comfort of merchants and troops. He acted upon these laws and it was proved by experience that they became the means of procuring tranquillity for the classes above mentioned. Sher Shah often said, "It behoves kings to inscribe the page of their history with the characters of religion, that their servants and subjects may love religion; for kings are partakers in every act of devotion and worship which proceeds from the priests and the people. Crime and violence prevent the development of prosperity. It behoves kings to be grateful for the favour that the Lord has made his people subject to them, and therefore not to disobey the commandments of God."

Sher Shar attended to every business concerning the administration of the kingdom and the revenues, whether great or small, in his own person. Nor did he permit his temporal affairs to be unmixed with devotion; day and night he was employed in both works. He had his dependent in waiting to awake him when two-thirds of the night were passed; and bathing himself every night he employed himself in prayer and supplication until the fourth watch. After that he heard the accounts of the various officers, and the ministers made their reports of the work to be done in their respective departments, and the orders which She Shah gave they recorded for their future guidance, that there might be no necessity for inquiry in future. When the morning had well broken, he again performed his ablutions, and with a great assembly went through his obligatory devotions, and afterwards read the *Musta'ab-i 'ashr,* and other prayers. After that his chiefs and soldiers came to pay their respect, and the "heralds" (*nakibs*) called out each man by name, and said: "Such and such a one, the son of such a one, pays his respects." One full hour after sunrise, that is to say about the first hour of the day, he performed the *Namaz-i-i shrak.*[95] After this, he inquired of his chiefs and soldiers if any of them had no *jagir,* that he might assign them one before entering on a campaign; and said that if any asked for a *jagir* while engaged in a campaign he should be punished. After that he asked if there were any who were oppressed or evil treated, that he might right them, for Sher Shah was adorned with the jewel of justice, and he oftentimes remarked, "Justice is the most excellent of religious rites, and it is approved alike by the kings of infidels and of the faithful." .... So he employed himself in personally discharging the administration of the kingdom, and divided both day and night into portions for each separate business, and suffered no sloth or idleness to find its way to him. "For," said he, "it behoves the great to be always active, and they should not consider, one account of the greatness of their own dignity and loftiness of their own rank, the affairs and business of the kingdom small or petty, and should place no undue reliance on their ministers. .... The corruption of ministers of contemporary princes was the means of my acquiring the worldly kingdom I possess. A king should not have corrupt *vakils* or

[95] These as well as some other of the observances noted above are supererogatory.—See *Kanun-i Islam,* p. 55.

wazirs: for a receiver of bribes is dependent on the giver of bribes; and one who is dependent is unfit for the office of *wazir,* for he is an interested personage; and to an interested person loyalty and truth in the administration of the kingdom are lost.''

When the young shoot of Sher Shah's prosperity came into bearing, he always ascertained the exact truth regarding the opprcsed, and the suitors for justice; and he never favoured the oppressors, although they might be his near relations, his dear sons, his renowned nobles, or of his own tribe; and he never showed any delay or lenity in punishing oppressors. . . . Among the rules which Sher Shah promulgated, and which were not before known in the world, is the branding of horses;[96] and he said he ordered it on this account, that the rights of the chiefs and their soldiers might be distinct,

[96] But the *Tarikh-i Khan Jahan* (MS., p. 187) says, that the practice was introduced by Sultan Sanjar, and that the example was followed by other Sultans; that in Hindustan, it was observed by 'Alau-d din Khilji, and that Sher Shah merely renewed his ordinance. Abu-l Fazl contemptuously remarks, that he sought the applause of future generations, by mere revivals of 'Alau-d din's regulations which he had read of in the *Tarikh-i Firoz Shahi*. Sher Shah was such an admirer of the *dagh* system that men, as well as cattle, on his register, had to submit to it. The *Tarikh-i Daudi,* (MS., p. 236) says that even the sweepers had the royal brand impressed on them; it omits to say on what part of the body. Allusion, however, may be made only to the horses of the sweepers, though it seems improbable that such a class should have had any. The passage in the *Waki'at-i Mushtaki* (MS., p. 99) runs thus: "Even in the Haram establishment he gave a salary to no one unless his horses were branded, in so much that even a sweeper caused the stamp to be applied. This work, as usual, is the source of the information in the *Tarikh-i Daudi*, and all the trivial anecdotes which follow on the subject of the *dagh* are the same in both.

and that the chiefs might not be able to defraud the soldiers of their rights; and that every one should maintain soldiers according to his rank (*mansab*), and should not vary his numbers. "For," said he, "in the time of Sultan Ibrahim, and afterwards, I observed that many base nobles were guilty of fraud and falsehood, who, at the time when their monthly salary was assigned to them, had a number of soldiers; but when they had got possession of their *jagirs*, they dismissed the greater number of their men without payment, and only kept a few men for indispensable duties, and did not even pay them in full. Nor did they regard the injury to their master's interests, or the ingratitude of their own conduct; and when their lord ordered a review or assembly of their forces, they brought strange men and horses, and mustered them, but the money they put into their own treasuries. In time of war they would be defeated from paucity of numbers, but they kept the money, and when their master's affairs became critical and disordered, they, equipping themselves with this very money took service elsewhere; so from the ruin of their master's fortunes they suffered no less. When I had the good fortune to gain power, I was on my guard against the deceit and fraud of both chiefs and soldiers, and ordered the horses to be branded, in order to block up the road against these tricks and frauds; so that the chiefs could not enertain strangers to fill up their ranks." Sher Shah's custom was this, that he would not pay their salary unless the horses were branded, and he carried it to such an extent that he would not give anything to the sweepers and women servants about the palace without a brand, and they wrote out descriptive rolls of the men and horses and brought them before him, and he himself compared the rolls when he fixed the monthly salaries, and then he had the horses branded in his presence.

After the *Namaz-i ishrak,* he went through various

business; he paid each man separately, mustered his old troops, and spoke to the newly-enlisted men himself and questioned the Afghans in their native tongue. If any one answered him accurately in the Afghan tongue, he said to him, "Draw a bow" and if he drew it well, he would give him a salary higher than the rest, and said, "I reckon the Afghan tongue as a friend." And in the same place he inspected the treasure which arrived from all parts of the kingdom, and gave audience to his nobles or their *vakils*, or to *zamindars*, or to the envoys of the kings of other countries, who came to his victorious camp; or he heard the reports which came from the nobles who were his *'amils*, and gave answers to them according to his own judgment and the *munshis* wrote them. When two hours and a half of the day were over, he rose up and eat his breakfast with his *'ulama* and holy men, and after breakfast he returned and was engaged as before described till mid-day. At mid-day he performed the *kailula* (which is a supererogatory act of devotion), and took a short repose. After his rest he performed the afternoon devotions in company with a large assembly of men, and afterwards employed himself in reading the Holy Word. After that he spent his time in the business described above; and whether at home or abroad, there was no violation of these rules.

The rules for the collection of revenue from the people and for the prosperity of the kingdom, were after this wise; There was appointed in every *pargana*,[97] one *amir*, one God-fearing *shikkdar*, one treasurer, one *karkun* to write Hindi, and one to write Persian; and he ordered his governors to measure the land every harvest, to collect the revenue according to the measurement, and in proportion to the produce, giving one share to the cultivator, and half a share to the *mukaddam*; and

[97] The *Waki-at-i Mushtaki* has this passage, and states that the *parganas* were 116,000 in number.

fixing the assessment with regard to the kind of grain, in order that the *mukaddams* and *chaudharis* and *'amils* should not oppress the cultivators, who are the support of the prosperity of the kingdom. Before his time it was not the custom to measure the land, but there was a *kanungo* in every *pargana*, from whom was ascertained the present, past and probable future state of the *pargana*. In every *sarkar* he appointed a chief *shikkdar* and a chief *Munsif*, that they might watch the conduct both of the *'amils* and the people; that the *'amils* should not oppress or injure the people, or embezzle the king's revenue; and if any quarrel arose among the king's *'amils* regarding the boundaries of the *parganas*, they were to settle it, that no confusion might find its way amongst the king's affairs. If the people, from any lawlessness or rebellious spirit, created a disturbance regarding the collection of the revenue, they were so to eradicate and destroy them with punishment and chastisement that their wickedness and rebellion should not spread to others.

Every year, or second year, he changed his *'amils*, and sent new ones, for he said, "I have examined much, and accurately ascertianed that there is no such income and advantage in other employments as in the government of a district. Therefore I send my good old loyal experienced servants to take charge of districts, that the salaries, profits, and advantages, may accrue to them in preference to others; and after two years, I change them, and send other servants like to them, that they also may prosper, and that under my rule all my old servants may enjoy these profits and advantages, and that the gate of comfort and ease may be opened to them."

And this amount of forces fully equipped and stored came yearly to the king's presence. His whole army was beyond all limit or numbering, and it increased every day. The rule regarding the army for guarding the kingdom from the disturbances of rebels, and to keep down and to repress contumacious and rebellious *zamindars,* so that no one should think the kingdom undefended, and therefore attempt to conquer it, was as follows: Sher Shah always kept 150,000 horse and 25,000 footmen, either armed with matchlocks or bows, present with him, and on some expeditions took even more with him. Haibat Khan Niazi, to whom the title of Azam Humayun had been granted, had one force consisting of 30,000 horsemen in the neighbourhood of the fort of Rohtas, near to Balnath of the *jogis,* and held in check the country of Kashmir and of the Ghakkars. Dibalpur and Multan were committed to Fath Jang Khan, and in that (latter) fort much treasure was stored; and in the fort of Milwat (which Tatar Khan Yusufkhail built in the time of Sultan Bahlol) was stationed Hamid Khan Kakar, who held such firm possession of the Nagarkot, Jwala, Dihdawal, and Jammu hills, in fact the whole hill-country, that no man dared to breathe in opposition to him; and he collected the revenue by measurement of land from the hill people. The *sarkar* of Sirhind was given in *jagir* to Masnad Ali Khawas Khan, who kept in that *sarkar* his slave Malik Bhagwant, at the capital Dehli. Mian Ahmad Khan Sarwani was *amir,* and 'Adil Khan and Hatim Khan *shikkdar* and *faujdar.* And as the head-men and cultivators of the *sarkar* of Sambhal had fled from the oppression of Nasir Khan, Sher Shah sent there Masnad Ali 'Isa Khan, son of Masnad 'Ali Haibat Khan Kalkapur Sarwani, who had the title of Khan-i 'Azam, and was counsellor and adviser of Sultans Bahlol and Sikandar; and he said to him: "I have given to you the *parganas* of Kant, Gola, and Tilhar for your family and your old horsemen. Enlist five thousand new cavalry, for the *sarkar* of Sambhal is full of disaffected and riotous people, and the cultivators of that *sarkar* are for the most part rebellious and contumacious, and they are always given to quarrelling with and resisting their rulers."

When Masnad Ali Isa Khan came to that *sarkar*, he being a lion in valour and gallantry, so humbled and overcame by the sword the contumacious *zamindars* of those parts, that they did not rebel even when he ordered them to cut down their jungles which they had cherished like children, but cut them with their own hands, though drawing deep sighs of affliction; and they reformed and repented them of their thieving and highway robberies, and they paid in at the city their revenue according to the measurements. Sher Khan said: "By reason of these two Sarwanis, that is to say, 'Isa Khan and Mian Ahmad, I have no cause for anxiety from the *sarkar* or Dehli to the *sarkar* of Lucknow.

And Bairak Niazi, who was *shikkdar* of Kanauj so subjected the contumacious and highway plunderers inhabiting the *parganas* of Malkonsah, that no man dared to draw a breath in contravention of his orders. Bairak Niazi so established authority over the people of Kanauj, that no man kept in his house a sword, an arrow, a bow, or a gun, nay, any iron article whatever, except the implements of husbandry and cooking utensils; and if he ordered the head-men of any village to attend him, they obeyed his order, and dared not for one moment to absent themselves. The fear and dread of him was so thoroughly instilled into the turbulent people of those parts, that according to the measurement they paid their revenue to the treasurers.

And when the rebellion and disobedience of the zamindars who live in the parts about the banks of the rivers Jumna and Chambal became known to Sher Shah, he brought 12,000 horsemen from the Sirhind *sarkar*, and quartered them in the *pargana* of Hatkant and that neighbouhood, and they repressed the *zamindars* and cultivators of those parts; nor did they pass over one person who exhibited any contumacy. And in the fort of Gwalior, Sher Shah kept a force to which were attached 1,000 matchlockmen. In Bayana, he left a division, besides a garrison of 500 matchlocks; in Rantambhor, another division, besides 1,600 matchlockmen; in the fort of Chitor, 3,000 matchlockmen;[98] in the fort of Shadmabad, or Mandu, was stationed Shujat Khan, with 10,000 horse and 7,000 matchlocks. He had his *jagirs* in Malwa and Hindia. In the fort of Raisin a force was stationed, together with 1,000 artillerymen; and in the fort of Chunar another force also, with 1,000 matchlockmen; and in the fort of Rohtas, near Bihar, he kept Ikhtiyar Khan Panni, with 10,000 matchlockmen; and Sher Sah kept treasures without number or reckoning in that fort. And he kept a force in the country of Bhadauria,[99] and another under Khawas Khan and 'Isa Khan in the country of Nagor Judhpur and Ajmir; another in Lucknow, and one in *sarkar* Kalpi. The kingdom of Bengal he divided into parts and made Kazi Fazilat *amir* of that whole kingdom. And in every place where it served his interests, he kept garrisons.

After a time he used to send for the forces which had enjoyed ease and comfort on their *jagirs*, and to send away in their stead the chiefs who had undergone labour and hardship with his victorious army. He ap-

[98] The *Tarikh-i Daudi* (MS., p. 229) says he had 8,000 matchlockmen in his service. He adds, that 1,600 were stationed in Chitor, 500 in Rantambhor, 1,000 in Bayana, 2,000 in Gwalior, and a due proportion in every other fort. Whether all these are included in the 8,000, or the 8,000 were a mere personal guard, is not plain. In no single instance does the enumeration correspond with that of our author.

[99] It is to be regretted that the MSS. show a want of concurrence in the enumeration of these forces. The *Tarikh-i Daudi*, in the passage quoted above, says that there was also maintained a body of footmen, acting singly and independently, called *paiks*; and 113,000 horsemen distributed throughout the parganas for the protection of the district forts.

pointed courts of justice in every place, and always employed himself in founding charities, not only for his lifetime, but even for after his death. May glory and blessings be upon his eminent dignity! For the convenience in travelling of poor travellers, on every road, at a distance of two *kos,* he made a *sarai;* and one road with *sarais* he made from the fort which he built in the Panjab to the city of Sunargaon, which is situated in the kingdom of Bengal, on the shore of the ocean. Another road he made from the city of Agra to Burhanpur, which is on the borders of the kingdom of the Dekhin, and he made one from the city of Agra to Judhpur and Chitor; and one road with *sarais* from the city of Lahore to Multan. Altogether he built 1,700 *sarais*[100] on various roads; and in every *sarai* he built separate lodgings, both for Hindus and Musulmans, and at the gate of every *sarai* he had placed pots full of water, that any one might drink; and in every *sarai* he settled Brahmans for the entertainment of Hindus, to provide hot and cold water, and beds and food, and grain for their horses; and it was a rule in these *sarais,* that whoever entered them received provision suitable to his rank, and food and litter for his cattle, from Government. Villages were established all round the *sarais.* In the middle of every *sarai* was a well and a *masjid* of burnt brick; and he placed an *imam* and a *mua'zzin* in every *masjid,* together with a custodian (*shahna*), and several watchmen; and all these were maintained from the land near the *sarai.* In every *sarai* two horses were kept, that they might quickly carry news.[101] I have heard that

[100] One MS. has 2,500 *Sarais.* The *Nawadiru-l Hikayat* (MS., p. 599) boldly says 2,500 *sarais* on the road from Bengal to the Indus alone. This arises from the double ignorance of rating that distance at 2,500 *kos* and a reckoning that there was a *sarai* at each *kos,* instead of at every second one.

[101] We shall see below, that they are said to have

Husain Tashtdar;[102] once, on an emergency, rode 300 *kos* in one day.[103] On both sides of the highway Sher Shah planted fruit-bearing trees, such as also gave much shade, that in the hot wind travellers might go along under the trees; and if they should stop by the way, might rest and take repose.[104] If they put up at a *sarai*, they bound their horses under the trees.

---

amounted to 3,400. The *Tarikh-i Khan Jahan* (MS. p. 186) adds: "In order that every day news might be conveyed to him from the Nilab and Agra, and the very extremities of the countries of Bengal." Sikandar Lodi has the credit of having established these *dak chaukis* before him.

[102] In some copies he is called "*Shikkdar*"; but in others, and very plainly in the two works quoted below, he is called "*Tashtdar*," or ewer-bearer, a member of the royal household.

[103] The *Waki' at-i Mushtaki* (MS., p. 97), followed by the *Tarikh-i Daudi* (MS., p. 225), has another account of this impossible feat, which would defy even a twenty-Osbaldistone power. Fifty miles an hour for twelve hours without intermission!!! "Husain Khan Tashtdar was sent on some business from Bengal. He went on travelling night and day. Whenever sleep came over him he placed himself on a bed (*chahar-pai*) and the villagers carried him along on their shoulders. When he awoke, he again mounted a horse, and went on his way. In this manner he reached Chitor from Gaur in three days; and think what a distance that is!" It is indeed, 800 miles, as the crow flies, over some of the most impracticable parts of India! Such senseless lying should be exposed; but the native mind is at present so constituted as to put implicit credence even in such an averment as this.

[104] The author of the *Muntakhabu-t Tawarikh* says that he himself saw the high road from Bengal to Rohtas, which was in many places so ornamented, after it had stood for fifty-two years. It is strange that, at this period, not a trace can be found of *sarai*, mosque, road, or tree.

Sher Shah also built a fort, Rohtas, on the road to Khurasan, to hold in check Kashmir and the country of Ghakkars, near the hill of Balnath Jogi, four *kos* from the river Behat, and about sixty *kos* from Lahore, and fortified and strengthened it exceedingly. There was never seen a place so fortified and immense sums were expended upon the work. I, 'Abbas Kalkapur Sarwani, author of the *Tuhfa-i Akbar Shahi,* have heard from the relators of the history of Sher Shah, that, when building this fort, stones were not procurable: The overseers wrote in their reports that stone was not procurable, or only pocurable at an enormous outlay. Sher Shah wrote back in reply, that his order should not be allowed to fail from avarice, and they should go on with the building though they paid for the stone its weight in copper. He caled that fort "Little Rohtas."[105]

The former capital city of Dehli was at a distance from the Jumna, and Sher Shah destroyed and rebuilt it by the bank of the Jumna, and ordered two forts to be built in that city, with the strength of a mountain, and loftier in height; the smaller fort for the governor's residence; the other, the wall round the entire city, to protect it;[106] and in the governor's fort he built a *jama masjid* of stone, in the ornamenting of which much gold, *lapis lazuli,* and other precious articles were expended. But the fortifications round the city were not completed when Sher Shah died. He destroyed also the old city of

---

His beautiful mausoleum at Sahsaram is still a stately object, standing in the centre of an artificial piece of water, faced by walls of cut stone.

[105] The *Tarikh-i Daudi* (MS., p. 236) says "New Rohtas," and adds, that "it cost eight *krors,* five lacs, five thousand and two and a half *dams* which means Bahlolis. All which is written over the gate of the fort."

[106] Literally, that it might be a "Jahan-panah," which was the name of one of the old cities of Dehli.

Kanauj, the former capital of the Kings of India, and built a fort of burnt brick there; and on the spot where he had gained his victory he built a city, and called it Sher Sur. I can find no satisfactory reason for the destruction of the old city, and the act was very unpopular. Another fort, that of Bohnkundal, he also built, and ordered another fort to be built in these hills, and called it "Sher Koh."[107] He said: "If my life lasts long enough, I will build a fort in every *sarkar*, on a suitable spot, which may in times of trouble become a refuge for the oppressed and a check to the contumacious; and I am making all the earthen-work *sarais* of brick, that they also may serve for the protection and safety of the highway."

For the protection of the roads from thieves and highway robbers, he made regulations as follows: He strictly impressed on his *'amils* and governors, that if a theft or robbery occurred within their limits, and the perpetrators were not discovered, then they should arrest the *mukaddams* of the surrounding villages, and compel them to make it good; but if the *mukaddams* produced the offenders, or pointed out their haunts, the *mukaddams* of the village where the offenders were sheltered were compelled to give to those of the village where the crime occurred the amount of restitution they had paid; the thieves and highway robbers themselves were punished with the penalties laid down in the holy law. And if murders should occur, and the murderers were not discovered, the *'amils* were enjoined to sieze the *mukaddams*, as detailed above, and imprison them, and give them a period within which to declare the murderers. If they produced the murderer, or pointed out where he lived, they were to let the *mukaddam* go, and to put the mur-

[107] There is a notice of the fort of Patna, which was built by him, among the Extracts from the *Tarikh-i Daudi*.

derer to death; but if the *mukaddams* of a village where the murder had occurred could not do this, they were themselves put to death; for it has been generally ascertained that theft and highway robberies can only take place by the connivance of these head-men. And if in some rare case a theft or highway robbery does occur within the limits of a village without the cognizance of the *mukaddam,* he will shortly make inquiry that he may ascertain the circumstances of it; for *mukaddams* and cultivators are alike thieves, and they bear to each other the intimate relations of kinsmen: hence either the *mukaddams* are implicated in thefts and highway robberies, or can ascertain who perpetrated them. If a *mukaddam* harbours thieves and robbers unknown to the governor, it is fit he should be punished, or even be put to death, that it may be a warning to others to abstain from similar acts.[108]

[108] The *Tarikh-i Daudi* (MS., pp. 231, 247) mentions two instances in illustration of this enforcement of village responsibility. One was, that a horse was stolen one night from Sher Shah's camp at Thanesar, for which all the *zamindars* for a circuit of fifty *kos* were summoned and held responsible, with the threat that if the thief and horse were not forthcoming within three days, the lives of every one of them would fall a sacrifice. Both were shortly produced, and the thief was immediately put to death. Another was a case in which a murder was committed near Etawa, on a piece of land which had long been disputed between the neighbourng villages. In this instance. it being impossible to fix upon the responsible village, Sher Shah directed that two men should be sent to cut down a tree which was near the spot where the murder was committed, with orders that any man who came to prohibit them should be sent in to him. A *mukaddam* of one of the villages came forward to remonstrate, and was dealt with accordingly. He was tauntingly asked, how he could know of a tree being cut down so far from his village, and yet not know of a man being cut down.

In the days of Sher Shah and of Islam Shah, the *mukaddams* used to protect the limits of their own villages, lest any thief or robber or enemy of their enemies, might injure a traveller, and so be the means of their destruction and death. And he directed his governors and *amils* to compel the people to treat merchants and travellers well in every way, and not to injure them at all; and if a merchant should die by the way, not to stretch out the hand of oppression and violence on his goods as if they were unowned; for Shaikh Nizami (may God be merciful to him!) has said: "If a merchant die in your country it is perfidy to lay hands on his property." Throughout his whole kingdom Sher Shah only levied customs on merchandize in two places, viz.: when it came from Bengal, customs were levied at Gharri (sikri-gali); when it came from the direction of Khurasan, the customs were levied on the borders of the kingdom; and again, a second duty was levied at the place of sale. No one dared to levy other customs either on the road or at the ferries, in town or village. Sher Shah, moreover, forbad his officials to purchase anything in the bazars except at the usual bazar rates and prices.

One of the regulations Sher Shah made was this: That his victorious standards should cause no injury to the cultivation of the people; and when he marched he personally examined into the state of the cultivation, and stationed horsemen round it to prevent people from trespassing on any one's field. I have heard from Khan-i 'azam Muzaffar Khan, who said he often accompanied Sher Shah, that he used to look out right and left, and (which God forbid!) if he saw any man injuring a field, he would cut off his ears with his own hand, and hanging the corn

All the inhabitants of the village were then seized and threatened with death, if the murderer were not produced within three days. Under these circumstances there was of course no difficulty in getting the culprit, or at least *a* culprit, who was forthwith executed!

(which he had plucked off) round his neck, would have him to be paraded through the camp.[109] And if from the narrowness of the road any cultivation was unavoidably destroyed, he would send *amirs,* with a surveyor, to measure the cultivation so destroyed, and give compensation in money to the cultivators. If unavoidably the tents of his soldiery were pitched near cultivation, the soldiers themselves watched it, lest any one else should injure it, and they should be blamed and be punished by Sher Shah, who showed no favour or partiality in the dispensation of justice. If he entered an enemy's country, he did not enslave or plunder the peasantry of that country, nor destroy their cultivation. "For," said he, "the cultivators are blameless, they submit to those in power; and if I oppress them they will abandon their villages, and the country will be ruined and deserted, and it will be a long time before it again becomes prosperous." Sher Shah very often invaded an enemy's country; but on account of his justice the people remained, and brought supplies to his army and he became known by the fame of his generosity and benevolence; and he was all day long occupied in scattering gold like the sun, in shedding pearls like a cloud; and this was the reason that the Afghans collected round him, and that the kingdom of Hindustan fell to him. And if any want befell his victorious army, he did not suffer one soldier or any poor helpless person to be in despair or utterly unprovided for, but gave them something for their subsistence. Every day he enlisted men, to give them a subsistence.

[109] The *Waki'at-i Mushtaki* (MS., p. 101) and the Tarikh-i Daudi (MS., p. 252) record a barbarous punishment inflicted on a camel-driver during a march in Malwa for plucking some green chick-pea. Sher Shah had a hole bored in his nose, and with his feet bound together he was suspended during a whole march with his head downward. "After that no one stretched out his hand upon corn!"

His kitchen was very extensive, for several thousand horsemen and private followers, who in the Afghan tongue are called "Fiahi", fed there; and there was a general order, that if any soldier or religious personage, or any cultivator, should be in need of food, he should feed at the king's kitchen, and should not be allowed to famish. And places for the dispensing of food to the poor and destitute, and to all necessitous persons, were established in the camp, that they might feed every one as above described. The daily cost of these meals, and of these places for the distribution of food, was 500 gold pieces (*ashrafis*).

It became known to him that the *imams* and religious persons had, since the time of Sultan Ibrahim, by bribing the *'amils,* got into their possession more land than they were entitled to hold; he therefore resumed their holdings, and investigating the cases himself, gave to each his right, and did not entirely deprive any man of his possessions. He then gave them money for their road expenses, and dismissed them. Destitute people, who were unable to provide for their own subsistence, like the blind, the old, the weak in body, widows and the sick, etc. to such he gave stipends from the treasury of the town in which they were resident, and giving them the expenses of their journey sent them away. And on account of the fraudulent practices of the religious personages (*imams*) he made this arrangement; he did not give the *farmans* directing the assignments to the religious personages themselves, but ordered the *munshis* to prepare the *farmans* relating to one *pargana,* and to bring them to him. Sher Shah then put them all into a letter and put his seal on it, and gave it to a trustworthy man of his own, and said to him, "Carry these *farmans* to such and such a *pargana.*" When the *farmans* came to the *shikkdar,* he first made over to the holy personages their stipends, and then gave the *farmans* into their possession. Sher Shah often said, "It is incumbent upon kings to give grants to *imams*: for the prosperity and populousness of the cities of Hind are dependent on the *imams* and holy men; and the teachers and travellers, and the necessitous, who can not come to the king, they will praise him, being supported by those who have grants; and the convenience of travellers and the poor is thereby secured, as well as the extension of learning, of skill, and religion; for whoever wishes that God Almighty should make him great, should cherish *'Ulama* and pious persons, that he may obtain honour in this world and felicity in the next."

To every pious Afghan who came into his presence from Afghanistan, Sher Shah used to give money to an amount exceeding his expectations, and he would say, "This is your share of the kingdom of Hind, which has fallen into my hands, this is assigned to you, come every year to receive it." And to his own tribe and family of Sur, who dwelt in the land of Roh, he sent an annual stipend in money, in proportion to the numbers of his family and retainers; and during the period of his dominion no Afghan, whether in Hind or Roh, was in want, but all became men of substance. It was the custom of the Afghans during the time of Sultans Bahlol and Sikandar, and as long as the dominion of the Afghans lasted, that if any Afghan received a sum of money, or a dress of honour, that sum of money or dress of honour was regularly apportioned to him, and he received it every year.

There were 5000 elephants in his elephant sheds, and the number of horses personally attached to him was never fixed, for his purchases and gifts of them were equally great; but 3400 horses were always kept ready in the *sarais* to bring intelligence every day from every quarter. 113,000 villages of Hind were included in the royal fisc.[110] He sent a *shikkdar* to each of his *parganas*,

[110] The original has "113,000 *parganas*, that is, villages;" but the *Waki'at-i Mushtaki* (MS., p. 98) says "113,000 *parganas*," without any such qualification.

which were all prosperous and tranquil, and there was not one place which was contumacious or desolated; the whole country was settled and happy; corn was cheap, nor during his time was there anywhere scarcity or fomine. His army was beyond all reckoning, and every day increased. For the enforcement of the regulations which he had published for the protection of the people, Sher Shah sent trusted spies with every force of his nobles, in order that, inquiring and secretly ascertaining all circumstances relating to the nobles, their soldiers, and the people, they might relate them to him; for the courtiers and ministers, for purposes of their own, do not report to the king the whole state of the kingdom, lest any disorder or deficiency which may have found its way into the courts of justice should be corrected.

I have heard from a trustworthy Afghan, who was with Shuja'at Khan, that when Sher Shah gave him the government of the kingdom of Malwa, at the time of assigning *jagirs*, his ministers said to him: "It is time to assign *jagirs* to the soldiery if it pleases your worship: keep a share for yourself from the portion assigned to the soldiery, and divide the rest among them. "Shuja'at Khan, from covetousness, agreed to his ministers' proposal. When his soldiers heard of it, 2000 of them, men of repute, both horse and foot, bound themselves together by an agreement, that if Shuja'at Khan permitted himself, from covetousness, to infringe their rights, they would represent the case to Sher Shah, who showed no favour in dispensing justice to any one on account of the amount of his followers, or on account of his kindred; that they would unanimously expose the innovations of Shuja'at Khan and his ministers, and that they would stand by and assist each other in good or evil and would not, for any worldly covetousness, scratch the face of friendship and alliance with the nail of disunion. After this agreement, they went on a march from Shuja'at Khan's forces, and sent a man of their own to him, saying: "Your Ministers do not give us the full rights which Sher Shah has bestowed on us, and it is contrary to his regulations that the soldiery should be defrauded; nay, the nobles ought rather to encourage the poor among their soldiery with presents, over and above their monthly pay, that in time of action they may serve them with earnestness and devotion. If you covet our rights, the door will be opened to enmity and mutiny, and your army and your forces will become disunited and dispirited, which will be the cause of disgrace to your ministers."

When Shuja'at Khan became aware of the request of his soldiers, he asked of his ministers what course it behoved him to pursue. They replied: "Two thousand cavalry have turned aside from the path of obedience, and you are lord of 10,000; if you fully satisfy these impudent persons, people will think you have done so for dread of Sher Shah. and dilatoriness and infirmity will find their way among the officers of your province and into the stability of your authority. It now becomes you to give a stern and peremptory reply, and such as shall leave no hope, so that others may not behave ill and may not disobey your commands." Covetousness sewed up the far-seeing eye of Shuja'at Khan's sagacity, and made him forgetful of the justice and watchfulness of Sher Shah. The soldiers, on receiving this harsh answer, took counsel together; some said that they ought to go to the presence of Sher Shah the Just; but some Afghans, who knew Sher Shah's disposition, and were moreover possessed of some share of prudence and sagacity, said to their friends, —"It is not proper to go ourselves to Sher Shah, for this reason: that he has posted us with Shuja'at Khan in this country of the Dekhin, and it is not right for us to move out of these parts without his orders. Let us send a *vakil* to Sher Shah, the protector of the oppressed, to represent the real circumstances of our case to him. Whatever he orders, let us act up to it; and if any business of the king's should meanwhile occur, it behoves us to exert ourselves in its settlement more than all others." At length the opinion of these Afghans was adopted by all, and they wrote an account of their state and sent it. Their *vakil* had not yet arrived when Sher Shah's spies reported the circumstances of Shuja'at Khan's quarrel with the 2000 remonstrants to Sher Shah. On hearing the news, Sher Shah was enraged, and sending for Shuja'at Khan's *vakil*, said to him, "Write to Shuja'at, and say: 'You were poor, and I ennobled you, and put under you Afghans better than yourself. Are you not satisfied with the revenue of your government, that you covet the rights of the soldiery? and are you without any shame before the people or any fear of God, and have you violated my regulations which I have enacted and promulgated for this very purpose, that the chief's rights and those of his soldiery might be distinct, and that the chiefs might respect the rights of the soldiers? If you were not a *protege* of my own, I would strip off your skin; but I pardon you this first fault. Do you, before their *vakil* reaches me appease your soldiery and give them a satisfactory answer, if not, and, their *vakil* comes and complains to me, I will resume your *jagirs,* and arrest and punish you severely. It does not behove nobles to disobey their master's orders, for this occasions the loss to him of his honour and authority.' "

When the *vakil's* letter reached Shuja'at Khan, he was exceedingly confounded and ashamed and disturbed with dread and apprehension; so reproaching his ministers, he said: "Your counsel has been the cause of disgrace and distress to me. How shall I show my face to the king?" Then going himself to the encampment of the 2000 remonstrants, he made many excuses for himself and appeasing the soldiery with promises and oaths that he would not do them any harm, and encouraging them with gifts and presents, brought them back to his own encampment. When the *vakil* of the soldiers turned back again from his journey, and came to Shuja'at Khan, the latter returned many thanks to heaven, and distributed much money to the poor and needy, and gave him a horse and a princely robe of honour. Sher Shah's authority, whether he was absent or present, was completely established over the race of Afghans. From the fear, either of personal punishment or of deprivation of office, there was not a creature who dared to act in opposition to his regulations; and if a son of his own, or a brother, or any of his relatives or kin, or any chief or minister, did a thing displeasing to Sher Shah, and it got to his knowledge, he would order him to be bound and put to death. All, laying aside every bond of friendship or respect, for the sake of the honour of the Afghan race, obeyed without delay his irresistible *farmans*.

I, the author of this relation, 'Abbas Kalkapur Sarwani, have heard that during the reign of Sher Shah, 'Azam Humayun Niazi was ruler of the Panjab and Multan and had a force of 30,000 horse under him. No other of Sher Shah's nobles had so great a force. Sher Shah sent his own nephew, Mubariz Khan, to govern the district of Roh, which was in the possession of the Niazis. Mubariz Khan ordered Khwaja Khizr Sambhali, chief of the Sambhals to give him a mud fort which he had built on the Indian (*i.e.*, eastern) bank of the river Sind. Mubariz Khan lived in this fort and the Sambhals were generally with him; indeed there was not a moment they were not employed in his service, and always obedient and submissive to him. The daughter of Allah-dad Sambhal had no equal in that tribe for beauty and comeliness. When Mubariz Khan heard the fame and renown of her beauty, he became, without having seen her, desparately in love with her, and the bird of rest and quiet flew out of his hand. Actuated by the pride of power, he took no account of clanship, which is much considered among the Afghans, and especially among the Rohilla men; and sending a confidential person to Allah-dad, demanded that he should give him his daughter in marriage. Allah-dad sent a civil reply, saying: "My lord is of high power and rank, and has many sons, and many high-born wives and women servants are in his female apartments; besides, my lord has been bred and brought up in Hindustan, and is possessed of delicate breeding and graceful accomplishments; my sons have the habits and manners of Roh. Alliance between myself and my lord is altogether unadvisable, as there is so wide a difference between us." When Mubariz Khan heard Allah-dad's answer, he was convulsed with exceeding anger, and set himself to injure and persecute the Sambhals, in the hope that they, being driven to extremities by his violence and oppression, might give him Allah-dad's daughter. From fear of Sher Shah, the Sambhals submitted to all the violence and oppression which Mubariz committed; but when it reached beyond all bounds of sufferance, Farid, Idris,[111] and Nizam, three illegitimate brothers of Allah-dad, said to Mubariz Khan,—"We three brothers have several daughters, and possess more influence in our tribe than Allah-dad. We will give you a daughter of any of us brothers you may wish, and do you then abstain from persecuting the Sambhals." Mubariz Khan replied:—"I do not require your daughters; give me Allah-dad's daughter."

When the Sambhals perceived that Mubariz Khan desired a thing which could never come to pass, they said undisguisedly to him,—"Intermarriages have continually taken pace between our families and yours, but always those of pure descent have intermarried with those of pure descent, and the illegitimate with the illegitimate. Although, with regard to your station in life, such a marriage is not an equal one, yet, as the mother of us three was, as yours was, a slave, and respecting the royal authority, we have agreed to our daughters being given in marriage to you, in order that the rust of quarrel and

[111] This name is doubtful.

contention might be effaced from between us. To this you have not consented, which we much regret; do not act in opposition to the fear of God and the customs of the Afghans. Allah-dad is of pure birth, and he never will be compelled to connect himself with you by force and violence, or from fear of you; do not entertain so vain a desire." When Mubariz Khan heard these words, from presumption, arrogance, and the pride of power, his wrath overpowered him; he gave way to anger and enmity, and hastened to persecute the Sambhals; and, on account of his hatred without any fault of theirs, laid waste their village and their property, and made prisoners of many of the inhabitants. Among these he carried off to his own house the daughter of Kheru, who was a dependent of Allah-dad, and filled the post of *shahna* among the Sambhals. The chiefs of the Sambhals came in a body to Mubariz Khan, and said: "The honour of our women and yours is one. Release the daughter of Kheru the *shahna*, and respect the honour of our women." But although the Sambhals humbly and earnestly entreated him, he would not listen to them, for his predestined time was near at hand. When the Sambhals were driven to despair, they said to Mubariz Khan:—"You were born in Hindustan, and do not understand the habits of the Afghans. The crane has never yet overpowered or domineered over the hawk. We have paid the reverence due to the king and to yourself. Leave us alone, and do not oppress and injure us beyond all bounds, and let this helpless one go free." Mubariz Khan in a passion replied:—"You talk of the honour of this dependent of yours; you will know what it is when I tear Allah-dad's daughter by force from her house, and bring her away." The chiefs of the Sambhals fell into a passion also, and said to Mubariz Khan:—"Have respect to your own life, and do not step beyond your own bounds. If you so much as look towards our women, we will slay you; though, in return for your life, they will put several of our chiefs to death." Mubariz Khan, on hearing this angry reply of the Sambhals, told his Hindustani door-keepers to beat the chiefs of the Sambhals out of his house, for they were insulting him. When the Hindustani door-keepers lifted up their sticks to beat the Sambhals out of the house, a tumult arose. The gallant Sambhals, who had, by Mubariz Khan's violence and oppression, been driven to extremities, grew enraged, and, in the twinkling of an eye, killed Mubariz Khan and most of his followers.

When Sher Shah heard the news, he wrote to 'Azam Humayun sayings:—"The Surs are a tribe the least quarrelsome of the Afghans, and if every Afghan was to kill a Sur not one would be left in the world. The Sambhals are of your own tribe. Do you bring them to order, and chastise them, that they may not set a bad example to others, and may refrain from killing their governors for the future." When this order reached 'Azam Humayun Niazi, he collected an army against the Sambhals. They hearing that 'Azam Humayun was coming in person against them, left their country, and took to the hills, where they occupied fortified positions, intending to go with their families to Kabul.

When 'Azam Humayun heard that it was the intention of the Sambhals to go to Kabul, he was overwhelmed with anxiety and grief, and took counsel with his people, saying:—"The Sambhals are my brethren, and a numerous tribe and race: we cannot seize them by force. If they go to Kabul, Sher Shah will think that I have been negligent in seizing them, and that they have escaped from these parts by my connivance. We must get hold of them by some stratagem or contrivance." He sent his *vakil* to them, and said:—"I have ascertained you are not to blame. You were much injured and oppressed by Mubariz Khan. I will send you to Sher Shah, and beg him to forgive your fault. According to the Afghan custom, the Niazis shall give several of their daughters in marriage to the Surs, or Sher Shah may put to death two or three of your chiefs. It is not fitting that the whole tribe should be exiled, and compelled to go to other countries." The Sambhals wrote in their reply:—"We are in difficulties. If the Surs come to fight with us, we will do our best against them, that it may be remembered in the world, how the Niazis combated, and how they went into exile! If you come and fight with us, on both sides Niazis will be killed; and if we are cast out, you will even then be disgraced—for it was your own tribe who were driven out, and you had no pity. But if you will bind yourself by promises and oaths, that you will not seek to injure or persecute us, we will come in and make our submission. 'Azam Humayun replied: "Have I no regard for my kin, that I should injure or persecute you?" So 'Azam Humayun made the most solemn promises and oaths to the Sambhals; and the whole tribe, with their wives and families came to him. When he saw that he had deceived the whole tribe of Sambhals, and that they had come in with their wives and families, he took measures to prevent their escape, and slew 900 persons. While he was putting them to death, the Niazis said to several of their friends among the Sambhals, "We will let you escape, fly!" But the Sambhals maintained the Afghan honour, and said:—"It is better to die with our wives and families than to live dishonoured; for it is well known proverb, 'The death of a whole tribe is a solemn feast.'" When 'Azam Humayun had slain most of the Sambhals, he sent their wives and families to Sher Shah. Sher Shah, who wished no man evil, disapproved of 'Azam Humayun's cruelty, and said: "Never before has such a shameful thing been done among the race of Afghans; but 'Azam Humayun in fear of the King has slain so many of his own tribe. It is only from his affection for the King that he would thus uselessly shed so much blood of his own tribe." He had intended to remove 'Azam Humayun from his government of the Panjab, but had no time before he was glorified in martyrdom. After his death, 'Azam Humayun displayed great loyalty, which shall be narrated in its proper place.

From the day that Sher Shah was established on the throne, no man dared to breathe in opposition to him; nor did any one raise the standard of contumacy or rebellion against him; nor was any heart-tormenting thorn produced in the garden of his kingdom; nor was there any of his nobles or soldiery, or a thief or a robber, who dared to direct the eye of dishonesty to the property of another, nor did any theft or robbery ever occur in his dominions. Travellers and wayfarers, during the time of Sher Shah's reign, were relieved from the trouble of keeping watch: nor did they fear to halt even in the midst of a desert. They encamped at night at every place, desert or inhabited, without fear; they placed their goods and property on the plain, and turned out their mules to graze, and themselves slept with minds at ease and free from care, as if in their own house; and the *zamindars,* for fear any mischief should occur to the travellers, and that they should suffer or be arrested on account of it, kept watch over them. And in the time of Sher Shah's rule, a decrepit old woman might place a basket full of gold ornaments on her head and go on a journey, and no thief or robber would come near her, for fear of the punishments which Sher Shah inflicted. "Such a shadow spread over the world, that a decrepit person feared not a Rustam." During his time, all quarrelling, disputing, fighting, and turmoiling, which is the nature of the Afghans, was altogether quieted, and put a stop to throughout the countries of Roh and of Hindustan. Sher Shah in wisdom and experience, was a second Haidar. In a very short period he gained the dominion of the country, and provided for the safety of the highways, the administration of the government, and the happiness of the soldiery and people. God is a discerner of righteousness!

THE END